CROSSING CULTURES

IN MENTAL HEALTH

**Edited by Diane R. Koslow
and Elizabeth Pathy Salett**

Washington, DC

Volume 1

Published by SIETAR International (The International Society
for Education, Training and Research)
1505 Twenty-second Street, NW
Washington, DC 20037 USA
(202) 296-4710

First Edition

Copyright © 1989 by
International Counseling Center

ISBN: 0-933934-15-7

Manufactured in the United States of America

10 9 8 7 6 5 4 3 2 1

Table of Contents

iii

Foreword

Crossing Cultures in Mental Health represents a new dimension in the field of cross-cultural counseling and training, bringing together perspectives pertaining to refugee, immigrant, and sojourner populations. The focus is thus on cultural *transitions* and the multiple and complex emotional and mental adjustment processes associated with movement from one culture into another. Cultural groups have concepts of "mental health" that are sometimes very different from one another. Yet there are consistencies that are common across numerous cultural and ethnic boundaries, and it is finding those bridges that allows the acculturation process to begin. Here lies the commitment of cross-cultural counseling.

Successful completion of the passage from one culture to another involves several stages, any of which has the potential to produce mental health problems. Refugees and immigrants typically face tremendous stresses even before they leave their own countries. They usually experience economic privation, hunger, human rights violations, and in many war-torn areas, torture, both physical and psychological. Once they have fled from their countries, these persons generally are moved or move several more times before settling into permanent relocation, a course of events that opens them to the vulnerabilities associated with inadequate housing, food shortages, and family breakups. Even sojourners, travelers who have chosen to work or study in another country temporarily and who have not undergone the wrenching debacles of war or political unrest, are not immune to the emotional distress of cultural adjustment. They, too, frequently fall victim to culture shock, a severe psychological disorientation manifested in a variety of pronounced behavioral and emotional changes. Irritability, hostility, inability to work effectively, depression, withdrawal, and psychosomatic illnesses may seize those whose cultural adjustment is less than complete.

Clearly, the process of cultural transition, especially if accompanied by other crises, presents many obstacles and is often fraught with confusion and pain. Yet, many people who survive the passage are not scarred for life as we frequently assume. On the contrary, the human spirit has remarkable capacity for healing, for triumphing over considerable odds and tremendous stresses. I have called those who do triumph "victorious personalities," people who have developed special character traits as a result of their stresses and adaptations. They emerge from their experience with resilience and with survivor merit, rather than survivor guilt, for they have amassed a set of skills that enable them not merely to survive but to transform themselves in the process. Such persons possess a special sense of self-esteem, and often they go forward to help others.

v

Their victories are ones they have struggled to achieve. And no matter what challenges life presents to them thereafter, they have a knack for thriving.

While most survivors of major cultural transitions carry the seeds of survivor merit with them, some are not able to realize their full potential as victorious personalities without the assistance of mental health professionals. As the authors of the following chapters attest, treating and counseling culturally displaced clients require special skills in understanding, patience, and appropriate techniques, in addition to knowledge of their clients' experiences.

I am certain that *Crossing Cultures in Mental Health* will be of great value in helping those who serve a culturally diverse population to negotiate the many psychological dimensions of cultural transitions. It is my hope that this volume will also challenge us to extend our understanding of the impact of cultural transitions on that elusive inner dimension—the sense of well-being—that makes the struggle of life worth it or not.

Gail Sheehy
New York

Gail Sheehy, an author and journalist, is known for her best sellers, *Passages, Pathfinders,* and *Spirit of Survival.* She is currently writing political profiles on national and international leaders for *Vanity Fair* magazine.

Introduction

Since its infancy, cross-cultural counseling has had to justify its existence and define its parameters. Much of the early work in the field focused on making the case that mental health treatment had failed to adequately serve the needs of Black Americans, Hispanics, and other ethnic minorities. The large influx of refugees and immigrants to the United States in the 1980s has underscored the importance of the field and encouraged the search for a conceptual framework as well as treatment procedures and techniques that are culturally appropriate for this country's increasingly multiethnic and multicultural society.

This book is addressed to mental health professionals, trainers, and others who work in the field of cross-cultural counseling. Its goal is to provide the reader with suggestions for improving skills in cross-cultural communication and to address specific issues of relevance in work with refugee, immigrant, and sojourner populations.

Communication is a vital component in the delivery of mental health services, and culture plays an integral part in shaping the way a service provider thinks, feels, listens, gestures, interprets, and speaks. In Part One, *Cross-Cultural Communication,* Katharine G. Baker describes an experiential training model in which participants are challenged to explore and sharpen their awareness of their own cultural biases and values. Orlando L. Taylor then discusses some of the cultural assumptions that may prevent effective cross-cultural dialogue in the counseling situation and, in turn, may lead to distortions in service delivery.

In Part Two, *Cross-Cultural Counseling,* a number of specific issues faced by immigrants and refugees are discussed. Immigrants, who typically come to this country seeking a better future or to join other family members, tend to experience less trauma than refugees, but they too must often cope with loss, readjustment, and in many cases, discrimination. For most refugees—who are forced to immigrate to another country to escape war, famine, economic hardship, or persecution—the departure from their homeland and their subsequent relocation are enormously traumatic. Many of them endure imprisonment, repeated relocations, rape, torture, robbery, and the loss of family and friends, as well as their livelihoods and homes.

For the counselor, the issues faced by immigrants tend to be more generically cross-cultural and emphasize the acquisition of culture-specific information and the provision of culturally relevant services. Lillian Comas-Díaz begins this part of the book by emphasizing the heterogeneity and cultural diversity of Hispanic immigrants, while drawing on their common cultural heritage and the similarity of values and communication styles. Dennis J. Hunt then turns to issues commonly faced by refugees. He describes the difficulties that Southeast Asian refugees typically experience prior to and upon arrival in the United States and proposes concrete ways to make the counseling experience more useful to such clients. Manuel Orlando García and Pedro F. Rodríguez explore the psychological effects of torture and political repression on Argentinian and Salvadoran victims and their families, and suggest a multidisciplinary approach to treating clients who are suffering from post-traumatic stress disorder. Kim Oanh Cook and Elizabeth M. Timberlake examine the special needs of Vietnamese immigrants, many of whom have lived here for more than a decade. They outline the typical adaptation process of refugees over a twelve-year period and provide suggestions for building a long-term support system. In the final chapter on cross-cultural counseling, Richard F. Mollica discusses clinical and policy issues affecting the development of effective mental health services for traumatized refugee patients and challenges mental health professionals to recognize and confront these needs.

Part Three, *Working with Sojourners,* addresses issues facing individuals and families who have chosen to reside temporarily in another country. Students, diplomatic and military personnel, and persons employed by multinational companies or international organizations who live abroad for a period of time often must cope with culture shock and culture fatigue while abroad, as well as adjustment difficulties upon returning home. Sandra Mumford Fowler and Fanchon Silberstein describe a training format to prepare families for overseas living. Their model highlights characteristics common to healthy family communications, which they suggest are the same factors that predict success in cross-cultural adjustment. David J. Bachner and Sharon K. Rudy conclude the book with an example of how institutional factors can intervene in the counseling process. Using the case of a foreign exchange student, they develop a framework for recognizing the complicated dynamics inherent in providing cross-cultural counseling within an agency setting.

In sum, this book touches on many of the most important issues in cross-cultural counseling and training today. The early works of Paul Pedersen, Amado Padillo, Derald Sue, and others have paved the way for establishing the field as one that is valid and empirically based. We are now at a point where we are more able to define the need for effective services to ethnic minority clients and to identify treatment procedures and techniques that are culturally relevant. Clearly, we must continue to fully explore and develop this new discipline. It is my hope that *Crossing Cultures in Mental Health* will both advance the knowledge base and stimulate new interest in this emerging field of inquiry.

I would like to extend my thanks to the authors of these chapters for their time and dedication to this project, and to Marty Thomson and Linda Camino for their helpful suggestions.

Elizabeth Pathy Salett
President, International Counseling Center
Washington, DC

April 1989

The International Counseling Center provides cross-cultural counseling, training, and education to individuals, families, and organizations through a network of highly qualified clinicians and consultants. It is a non-profit organization founded in 1983.

International Counseling Center
3000 Connecticut Avenue, NW
Suite 138
Washington, DC 20008

About the Editors and Contributors

The Editors:

Diane R. Koslow, Ph.D., is a consultant to the U.S. Public Health Service and the International Counseling Center, and a licensed psychologist in private practice in Rockville, MD.

Elizabeth Pathy Salett, M.S.W., is president and founder of the International Counseling Center and a clinical social worker in private practice.

The Contributors:

David J. Bachner, Ph.D., is director of educational and program services and director of Asia/Pacific programs at Youth for Understanding in Washington, DC. A former exchange student and Peace Corps volunteer, he is active in NAFSA, SIETAR, and the American Psychological Association.

Katharine G. Baker, D.S.W., is a clinical social worker in private practice. She has lectured at Catholic University and Trinity College and has been a consultant to the Experiment in International Living and the U.S. Department of State.

Lillian Comas-Díaz, Ph.D., is a clinical psychologist and co-director of the Transcultural Mental Health Institute, Washington, DC. She is past director of the American Psychological Association's Office of Ethnic Minority Affairs.

Kim Oanh Cook, M.S.W., is executive director of the Mutual Assistance Association Consortium and former director of Project Bridge of the Alexandria (VA) Community Mental Health Center. She has a private practice and consults on cross-cultural topics.

Sandra Mumford Fowler, M.S., is past president of SIETAR International, and an independent trainer and consultant. A well-known lecturer and author, her most recent publication is entitled "Intercultural Simulation Games: Removing Cultural Blinders."

Manuel Orlando García, M.D., is an Argentinian-born board-certified psychiatrist with extensive cross-cultural and human rights experience. He is the host of the popular Spanish-language talk show, WADA a tu Lado.

Dennis J. Hunt, Ph.D., is director of Connections, Cross-Cultural Counseling and Foster Care Services, in Virginia. He is a consultant to the National Institute of Mental Health in refugee mental health, and has studied and taught in Portuguese and Brazilian universities.

Richard F. Mollica, M.D., a psychiatrist, is clinical director of the Indochinese Psychiatry Clinic, Department of Psychiatry, St. Elizabeth's Hospital, Brighton, MA. He is also director of the Harvard University program on Refugee Trauma, Harvard School of Public Health.

Pedro F. Rodríguez, M.D., is a child psychiatrist from El Salvador who has lived in the United States for several years. He is medical director of the James Weldon Johnson Counseling Center in New York City and serves as consultant to a self-help group of Salvadoran refugees.

Sharon K. Rudy, Ed.S, is director of counseling services at Youth for Understanding, Washington, DC. She develops materials and training programs on counseling systems worldwide and has worked with NAFSA, SIETAR, and AACD, among other educational institutions.

Fanchon Silberstein, M.A., former director of the Overseas Briefing Center for the Foreign Service Institute, is an independent trainer and consultant based in Washington, DC. She recently completed a manual for the Air Force on mobile families.

Orlando L. Taylor, Ph.D., is dean of the School of Communications at Howard University and an internationally recognized communications scientist. He is a widely published author who was the leading organizer of four World Congresses on Communication and Development in Africa and the African Diaspora.

Elizabeth M. Timberlake, D.S.W., is a professor at Catholic University, National Catholic School of Social Work. She has made numerous contributions in the fields of social work, child welfare, and education.

Part One

Cross-Cultural Communication

Chapter 1

A Workshop Model for Exploring One's Own Cultural Identity
Katharine G. Baker

Culture is always "a silent participant in the enterprise of psychotherapy" (Draguns, 1981). This chapter addresses some of the cultural incongruencies which frequently exist between mental health workers and their clients. It presents a model for a cross-cultural experiential training workshop which challenges participants to explore their own cultural values and biases, as well as those of their professions, and to heighten their awareness of the mixed values and biases they bring to their work with clients of diverse cultures.

Culture has been defined as the systems of meaning and values that shape human behavior (Kroeber & Parsons, 1958; Seelye, 1985). It can be expressed in a variety of contexts including ecological setting (rural, urban, suburban), philosophical or religious values, nationality, type of family organization, social class, occupation, and migratory patterns (Falicov & Hansen, 1983). In a multicultural society such as the United States, diverse cultural groups interact with each other, bringing diverse values, ideas, and other symbolic-meaningful systems to their interactions.

In large urban areas, mental health clinics are filled with people from many cultural backgrounds, including immigrants and refugees from distant lands as well as those who have migrated to the city from small farming communities in search of jobs. In many cases the cultural backgrounds of clinicians and their clients are very different.

The high dropout rate from mental health treatment in clinics across the country suggests that mental health professionals may be in need of better preparation both academically and personally, to work with clients from diverse cultural backgrounds. Misunderstanding, ignorance, racism, and insensitivity to cultural nuances are common theses in the literature on cross-cultural counseling (Brislin & Pedersen, 1976; Giordano, 1976; Green, 1982; Marsella & Pedersen, 1981; Pedersen, 1983; Seelye, 1985; Singer, 1987; Sue, 1981).

Most mental health workers come from middle-class backgrounds and expect their clients to be open, verbal, and psychologically minded. They tend to value verbal, emotional, and behavioral expressiveness. They believe that the development of insight is a sign of "cure" in a client (Sue, 1981).

Sensitivity to cultural varieties of self-expression, problem solving, and language is generally a neglected area in the education, training, and professional

3

supervision of mental health workers (Brislin & Pedersen, 1976; Pedersen, 1983).

The Workshop Model

The workshop model presented in this chapter is based on the premise that cross-cultural training should be (but is not) an integral part of all mental health academic curricula, at both the undergraduate and graduate levels. Moreover, the knowledge base for developing cross-cultural understanding should include not only information about specific cultures with which the student might be professionally engaged, but should also include an understanding of the generic dimensions into which all cultures fit (see Brislin & Pedersen, 1976; Singer, 1987; Spiegel, 1982; Spradley, 1979). Within this perspective, the student might become an expert on the emotional and relationship elements of specific ethnic groups, while also focusing on broader cultural issues—for example, the "fundamental cross-cultural requirements of being a family, such as the maintenance of marriages or the fundamentals of socializing children" (Montalvo & Gutierrez, 1983, p. 17).

Green (1982) describes this duality in cross-cultural study and education through an "emic-etic" dichotomy:

> An emic analysis is one which is based on localized, group-specific categories and which is intended to generate an "insider's" perspective of how the world is organized. Etic analyses are useful in making broad-scaled, cross-cultural generalizations or global statements. Emic analyses delineate the structure of a single culture in terms of the cognitive and behavioral categories which are specific only to that culture. Etic approaches normally obscure fine-textured detail in order to achieve generalizing power (p. 72).

The workshop model described in this chapter necessarily has an etic focus since it would be impossible to address the broad variety of emic issues in depth within the time constraints of a workshop (whether it lasts for an hour or a weekend). The workshop was formulated to provide a forum in which professional mental health workers can exchange ideas and practical techniques for improving mental health care across cultural boundaries. The workshop approach has some advantages over traditional academic approaches to cross-cultural education because of its intensity, its specificity, and its immediacy (Brislin & Pedersen, 1976).

An experiential workshop enables participants to internalize new information through the experience of living it, if even for a brief period. The participants themselves are the key to effective experiential education. Each participant comes to a workshop bringing two different psychological worlds: the inner world of perception, including personal goals, values, attitudes, and memories; and the outer world of life experience, including relationships, environments, and events. Middle-class American culture tends to separate these inner and outer worlds, defining them as subjective and objective aspects of experience respectively, and failing to observe their continuity. Despite this artificial dichotomy, an individual's two psychological worlds are closely related, with energy flowing between them continuously (see Janeway, 1977, p. 7).

An experiential workshop seeks to activate this flow of energy between the subjective and the objective. However, the workshop experience is only an initial step. Far more important is the participants' ability to understand the meaning of the experience and to formulate behavior and action based on that new understanding (see Janeway, 1977, p. 7). This clarification of meaning through experience is a particularly relevant training approach in the area of cultural awareness because so much of culture is connected with subjective perception and cannot be accessed except through the immediacy of interactive events.

The cross-cultural experiential workshop model described in this chapter has been tested on groups ranging in size from 30 to 90 participants. The participants have been mental health workers, including school counselors, therapists, employment counselors, and substance abuse coordinators. The remainder of the chapter will describe the workshop in terms of its goals, interactive norms, structural format, outcome planning, and evaluation. Specific units of time are not indicated for the workshop model since it can be adapted to the amount of time available. It should not, however, be undertaken in a time frame of less than 1-1/2 hours.

Goals of the Workshop

The primary goal of the workshop is to increase the sensitivity of participants to the cultural values and biases which they bring to their work with clients whose cultural backgrounds are different from their own.

Additional goals for each participant include the following:

o   *To acquire an understanding of culture*
    Participants will develop a clear understanding of the many generic components of culture.

o   *To enhance an awareness of behaviors, values/beliefs, and biases which derive from one's family of origin culture*
    Participants will have increased understanding of how their approaches to clients reflect the attitudes and beliefs of the families in which they grew up.

o   *To enhance an awareness of behaviors, values/beliefs, and biases which derive from professional training and experience*
Participants will increase their understanding of the aspects of their approaches to clients which reflect the attitudes and beliefs of the professions into which they have been trained.

o   *To acquire an understanding of the personal process of integrating one's family and professional identities*
As participants become aware of how their approaches to clients reflect a mix of family attitudes and professional attitudes, they will begin to incorporate the similarities and differences of those approaches into a smoother, more coherent balance.

o   *To acquire an experience of the loss incurred in cultural uprooting*
Participants will go through an exercise which will stir up feelings of anger and helplessness similar to those feelings experienced much more intensely by people going through a true cultural uprooting.

o   *To acquire skills to enhance the cultural self-integration of clients of different cultures*
As participants become more sensitive to integrating their own personal and professional biases, they will be able to help their clients to accomplish the same integration.

o   *To make a personal commitment to an action plan for continuing one's development of cultural awareness*
Participants will write down and then share with others their plans for putting what they have learned to work in their own job and family settings.

o   *To begin the development of a cross-cultural network among workshop participants*
Participants will share names, addresses, phone numbers, and professional experiences with each other.

Although these are not "researchable goals" with measurable outcome variables (Blake & Heslin, 1983; Brislin & Pedersen, 1976), they express the value-based intentions of this exploratory workshop model and may eventually be operationalized into measurable criteria for evaluation.

Interactive Norms

The workshop participants are encouraged to make calm, clear, autonomous, self-defining statements with regard to their personal cultural identity. They are also expected to listen to the personal statements of others with interest, acceptance, and openness to diversity.

When the workshop participants are asked to divide into smaller groups, the interactive norms of these small groups differ from those of therapy groups in which change is effected through the development of internal group cohesion. Group cohesion is not particularly appropriate to this workshop, although some degree of group cohesion will inevitably develop during the time that participants are together. This normal group tendency toward cohesion is particularly apparent when participants are switched from one small group to another at one point in the workshop. Rather than emphasizing group cohesion, this workshop is designed to help participants develop a sense of personal and cultural differentiation which they are able to articulate comfortably to others.

Description of the Workshop Model in Action

This workshop was most recently offered to a multidisciplinary group of approximately 30 participants as part of a large, two-day, cross-cultural symposium. Three hours were allotted to the workshop, which took place in a quiet, sunny, college classroom in downtown Washington, DC. The description which follows is based on that particular workshop.

Structural Format

The workshop is divided as follows:
o   self-introductions and definitions of culture discussed by the whole group;
o   four sets of questions which are discussed in small groups, with common themes reported back to the whole group; and
o   individual action plans.

Self-Introductions

In the initial self-introduction period, participants were asked to give their names and briefly (in one or two sentences) describe their ethnic/cultural identities. They were asked not to identify their work settings since the purpose in the introductions was to establish a sense of each participant's personal cultural identity apart from his or her professional identity. The leader of the workshop began by introducing herself, thereby serving as a role model in the expression of cross-cultural awareness and self-awareness for the participants.

This particular group included several men and women of African-American background who had grown up in southern inner-city and rural settings, a woman of mixed Italian and Polish background who had grown up in New England, four Vietnamese-American men and women, a Polish woman who had immigrated to the United States as a young adult, a self-described "army brat," a woman (wearing a sari) who had been born and lived most of her life in India, a man who was part African-American and part Cherokee Indian, two women who had grown up in close-knit Italian-American communities in large Eastern cities, a male Cambodian graduate student who had been in the United States since 1981, a woman from Ethiopia who had only recently arrived in the United States, several people who described themselves as WASPs, a woman who had grown up in the rural West, and a woman who defined herself as a "white, Unitarian, senior citizen."

As was apparent from the self-introductions, this group tended to define cultural identity in terms of nationality, race, and geography. Further discussion of the nature of culture led to a brainstorming effort, in which some of the following "cultural" categories were generated by the group and listed on a flip-chart:

Gender	Education
Habitat	Nationality
Personal history	Religion
Socioeconomic status	Geography
Community	Language
Art, music, drama	Food
Age	Parental occupation
Profession	Race

A discussion of the many categories considered to be expressive of culture could be entered into at this phase of the workshop, depending on the amount of time available to the workshop (see Spiegel, 1982, for further discussion of cultural categories).

This workshop group included race as a category expressive of culture, although many social theorists would agree with Green (1982), that "while perceived differences in race may be socially meaningful to the participants in a cross-cultural encounter, race as such has no standing as a scientific or analytical category. . . . Race is a social concept, not a biological one, and it serves no purpose other than to make and justify invidious distinctions between groups of people" (p. 6).

It is interesting that, as Pinderhughes (1979) has noted, being "Black" is frequently considered to be expressive of ethnic or cultural identity, whereas being "white" is not: "Identity for whites is (most often) viewed in terms of national origin, whereas identity for people of color is viewed in terms of race" (p. 313). In this particular workshop group, race had strong social and political, as well as cultural, meaning for Black and Asian participants.

Following the discussion of what categories constitute culture, the participants were divided into small groups of five to eight people. Participants were asked to join a group in which they did not know any of the other members. Each group selected a reporter (to take notes and to report back to the larger groups) and a time-keeper (to ensure that all group members had equal opportunity to express themselves).

Personal Cultural Identity

The leader of the workshop then presented the first series of questions for discussion. These questions were written on a flip-chart at the front of the room and were read to the whole group by the leader. Depending on the amount of time available, the questions can be answered by the participants in sequence or all together. In this workshop, each group member made a personal statement that included the answers to all three of the questions relating to personal cultural identity. The leader of the workshop "floated" from group to group, listening for common themes and areas of interest.

The first series of questions related to the participants' personal cultural identities:

1. What is your own cultural/ethnic background?
2. How did your family define this identity to you during your childhood?
3. How did your family relate to the surrounding community in terms of culture/ethnicity during your childhood?

After these questions had been answered by all the individuals within the small groups, the reporters presented to the larger group common themes they had noted in the answers. Some of the common themes which emerged were these:

o   I come from a strong family unit in which family values were expressed verbally as well as through behavior.

o   Although my family struggled with poverty, the importance of education and religion was emphasized.

o   In my family we were encouraged to be autonomous individuals. Individual differences were respected.

o   Racial conflict was paramount in my community. I was taught to avoid confrontation in order to survive.

o   As a child I had a very positive sense of my own culture as an island in the wider mainstream culture.

o   My family protected me from the community. They believed I could learn to deal with the negatives later in life.

o   We struggled, but we coped.

Many of the workshop participants described their earliest cultural experiences as "cocoon-like," as though their families and immediate cultural group folded protective wings around them, enabling them to grow strong before having to deal with the larger community which was often perceived as hostile or destructive. This view of family vs. larger community reflects the direction that Pinderhughes (1979) has explored when she asks social work students to focus on "the power relationships between your ethnic group and others" (p. 313). She notes that students often raise questions about social class in relation to ethnicity, theorizing that power derived from middle- or upper-class status diminishes the need for strong ethnic identity.

In these initial responses to questions about self and cultural identity, the participants listened to each other with interest, acknowledging the broad diversity of the group, both in terms of ethnicity and of early life experience. A tone of nonjudgmental interest and mutual acceptance was established early in the workshop.

Professional Cultural Identity

The workshop participants again broke into small groups to answer a series of questions having to do with professional identity:

1. How do you define your professional identity?
2. How did you acquire your sense of professional identity?
3. What are the key elements of your professional identity?
   o   Values/beliefs
   o   Status/community sanctions
   o   Characteristic behaviors
   o   Roles
   o   Communication styles

Again, after each participant answered these questions in the small groups, the recorders presented common themes to the larger group. In this case, most of the participants were mental health professionals, along with some employment counselors, school counselors, and teachers. Thus, most of them had acquired a sense of professional identity through completion of degree programs or graduate school courses, relationships with professional organizations, adherence to a professional code of ethics, reading of professional materials, and the acknowledgement of professionalism that they receive from clients, co-workers, and members of their communities.

The key elements of professional identity included a sense of expertise, roles learned during training, and open, verbal communication style. Professional behaviors were described as generally direct, authoritative, enabling, and assertive. Many aspects of professional culture identified in this workshop are similar to those described by Greenwood (1957) in his study of the attributes of professions.

Again the participants listened to each other respectfully throughout the personal statements and group reports. In this section of the workshop, there was much more commonality than in the first section, where striking differences had been apparent. Shared professional culture and identity provided a bond for people whose families of origin were very different. They were more connected to each other through adult life experience and learned values than they were through family culture.

Personal Cultural Integration—
and an Experiential Disruption

The workshop participants again divided into the same small groups to answer a third set of questions having to do with changes which occurred in themselves during the transition from being a child within a family culture to becoming an adult within a professional culture. The questions were as follows:

1. How have you integrated your cultural/ethnic identity with your professional identity?
2. What conflicts have arisen for you?
3. What changes have occurred in your sense of self?
4. How does stress or anxiety affect your sense of self?

As the participants were answering these questions in small groups, the leader went from group to group and asked one member of each group to change places with a designated member of another group. No explanation of these switches was given, and the groups continued their discussions of the assigned set of questions. Most of the groups neither said good-bye to their departing (switched-out) member nor greeted their new (switched-in) member, and the new members did not participate actively in this set of discussions.

When the full group reconvened, the leader asked those who had been switched to describe what the experience had been like for them. She then asked group members to describe their reactions to losing a group member and gaining a new member.

All the participants expressed anger at the leader for disrupting the small groups without explanation. Those who had been switched expressed a sense of loss and of unconnectedness with the new group. The other group members expressed feelings of sadness at losing particularly active individuals from their small groups and anger which was projected onto incoming members through a lack of welcome to them.

As the discussion progressed, it gradually became clear to the participants that the seemingly arbitrary disruption of the small groups had been an experiential exercise in cross-cultural transition and adjustment. While in no way approaching the trauma experienced by refugees and others who have no control over their moves from one culture to another, the movement of individuals from one group to another in this simple exercise did, in fact, arouse strong feelings of anger, confusion, frustration, scapegoating, and even brief disorientation— both among those who had been moved and those who had not. Participants were thus made aware of the forces toward small group cohesion (community/culture building) which had occurred in the very short time span of the workshop, even though the leader had specifically stated at the beginning that group cohesion was not a goal of the workshop.

The dramatic impact of this experiential exercise heightened the full-group discussion of the questions having to do with the self-integration of the participants' personal and professional cultures, particularly when their chosen career path took them in a direction leading away from family.

Considerable discussion ensued as to how professionalization affected one's closeness vs. distance from one's family. Several participants felt that they "could never go home again" because they had become so distant from their homes of origin. A sense of being a "transitional generation" in their families was powerful for those whose parents had not been professionals. Others felt that "home is in the head" and "you carry it wherever you go in life." Clearly members of the workshop were at different stages in their own personal integration of family and professional identities. Those who had grown up in middle-class, professional families were not necessarily closer to a personal integration of identity than those who had grown up in cultures where the contrasts were more striking.

Several participants said they felt a sense of continuity between their family's values and their own professional values, resulting in a deep sense of obligation to serve those who were less fortunate than they and a desire to give back what had been given to them when they were growing up. Others felt their professional culture built on their family culture, even though the two were quite different. These group members had not felt the need to cut themselves off from their families of origin in order to become professional, but instead felt enriched by this augmentation of self, which had carried over into their own adult family-making.

The sense of disruption, confusion, and anger which had occurred in the experiential exercise had also occurred for many participants in their transitions from child-in-family to adult-in-profession, but many had forgotten its intensity until they re-experienced it in the workshop. In answering the question "How does stress or anxiety affect your sense of self?" they were able to observe their self-functioning at a somewhat regressed level (scapegoating, confusion) in response to the stress of the small group disruption, and then to translate this self-observation into situations of more serious "real life" stress, particularly with regard to cross-cultural transitions.

Application to Work with Clients

The fourth set of questions was intended to help the participants make a practical translation of the lessons of the workshop into work with clients of diverse cultures:

1. What areas do you focus on with clients which emphasize a sense of "difference" for you?
2. What areas do you focus on with clients which emphasize a sense of commonality or universality in human experience?
3. In your work with clients from different cultures, how do you enhance their strengths and coping skills?
4. How does this relate to your own process of self-integration?

Following individual statements in small groups, these questions led to a large-group discussion of the themes addressed at the beginning of this chapter, including the usefulness of culture-specific vs. culture-universal (or emic vs. etic) approaches to cross-cultural training. There was considerable disagreement among participants about the relative values of these differing approaches; some stated that it would be unrealistic and narrowing to master the details of a few specific client cultures, while others felt that an exclusively generalist approach would inevitably miss important cultural nuances.

The role of the professional as a "culture broker" for the client (see McGoldrick, Pearce, & Giordano, 1982, p. 23) was also discussed. Many participants in the workshop actively undertook this role in their professional work as they assisted clients from different cultures in their adjustments to a new culture. Mastering the art of "switching" appeared to be an important part of this adjustment, since individuals who can flexibly switch between family culture and community culture can get along in the mainstream culture without losing the strength and identity which the family culture provides.

Some of the evocative comments of participants in this segment of the workshop include the following:

o A major cultural difference for me in working with refugee clients is that they won't talk about feelings.
o The whole family defers to the father, and I can't figure out what the others really think.
o Traditional dress is beautiful and exotic, and it's sad to realize that they'll never really adjust to our culture until they give it up.
o A mother is a mother the whole world over.
o My refugee clients carry around with them an experience of loss and grief and trauma that I can't even begin to understand.
o I think I am most helpful to my clients when I realize that, in spite of our differences, we have so much in common—we love our children, our families, our friends; we are striving to make something of our lives; we are open to learning; we are looking for spiritual meaning.
o In spite of all my professional training, I have always thought of my grandmother as one of the wisest people I know. My connection with her helps me to overcome the superficial differences which may exist between me and my clients.

Those workshop participants who had most effectively integrated their own family and professional identities tended to be most respectful of clients from diverse cultures. They were comfortable "coaching" clients to work on an acceptance of self which was concurrent with an ability to function at high levels both in the mainstream culture and at home.

Action Plans

At this point in the workshop the participants were asked to sit quietly for several minutes and come up with a short, personal plan of action with regard to their work in the cross-cultural field. Each action plan was to answer the following questions:

1. What specific actions can I take to understand my family-of-origin culture more deeply during the coming months and over the course of the coming year?
2. What specific actions can I take to integrate my family-of-origin culture and my professional culture in a way that will be more comfortable for me over the coming month and over the coming year?
3. What specific actions can I take with particular clients which will help me listen to them better and learn more from them about the experience of cultural transition?

Each participant was then asked to share his or her action plan with one other participant in the workshop, making a commitment to follow up on the plan with this other person at the end of one month and at the end of one year. Although the action plans are very personal, the participants' commitment to their plans is greatly reinforced by a quasi-public acknowledgement of their substance.

In attempting to better understand their family-of-origin culture, many of the participants planned to reconnect with older relatives through letters and visits, thus learning more about the experiences of these family members in making their own life adjustments.

Many of the action plans having to do with personal integrations of family-of-origin culture and professional culture acknowledged the importance of valuing the diversity of the participants' own experience and values. Several participants planned to keep a journal of personal reflections and observations about this inner process.

Action plans relating to the incorporation of personal cultural awareness into work with clients reflected the participants' work settings. Many of the mental health professionals in the workshop felt committed to action plans that would lead them in the direction of being more accepting of differences, and more tolerant and calm in acknowledging the long time frames required in cross-cultural transitions. Other professionals faced with the necessities of time-limited, task-focused work with clients expressed the same commitment to a change in attitude, a greater openness, and a valuing of diversity.

The workshop concluded with a general discussion and informal sharing, as participants wished, of aspects of specific action plans which might interest the full group. In addition, participants in the workshop were asked to share their work settings, addresses, and telephone numbers with each other so that the goal of cross-cultural networking might begin to be met.

Participants were also asked to complete a simple evaluation of the workshop; a brief questionnaire focused on teaching methodology and suggestions for future presentations.

Summary

The workshop participants began to acquire an understanding of the meaning of culture as they identified themselves to each other at the beginning of the session. They explored their own behaviors, values/beliefs, and biases which had derived both from their family-of-origin cultures and from their professional training and experience. They then began to acquire an understanding of the personal process of integrating family and professional identities. They were helped to experience (albeit superficially) the loss incurred in cultural uprooting when members were switched out of the small groups. They began to think about the skills which are required for enhancing cultural self-integration in clients of different cultures. Each participant made a personal commitment to an action plan for continuing development of cultural awareness. The participants also began the process of developing a professionally supportive, cross-cultural network amongst themselves.

Because of the brevity of the workshop, these goals could be achieved only in a preliminary sense. Nevertheless, the workshop stimulated much thought and encouraged the participants to commit themselves to increased cross-cultural awareness and sensitivity, both on a personal and professional level.

As a training model, the workshop can be developed by future facilitators in directions which will provide opportunities for participants to explore the interface between personal and professional cultures and its impact on their work with clients of diverse cultural backgrounds. Commitment to personal action plans and mutually supportive follow-up with fellow members of the workshop are key elements in the long-term effectiveness of this brief training model. It aspires to effect significant change in the delivery of mental health services to clients who have experienced major disruptions in their lives and who are searching for ways to stabilize themselves in a strange environment without losing their connection with the culture from which they have come.

References

Blake, F. B., & Heslin, R. (1983). Evaluating cross-cultural training. In D. Landis & R. W. Brislin (Eds.), *Handbook of intercultural training*. New York: Pergamon Press.

Brislin, R. W., & Pedersen, P. B. (1976). *Cross-cultural orientation programs*. New York: Gardner Press.

Draguns, J. G. (1981). Cross-cultural counseling and psychotherapy: History, issues, current status. In A. J. Marsella & P. B. Pedersen (Eds.), *Cross-cultural counseling and psychotherapy* (pp. 3-28). New York: Pergamon Press.

Falicov, C. J., & Hansen, J. C. (Eds.). (1983). *Cultural perspectives in family therapy*. Rockville, MD: Aspen Systems Corporation.

Giordano, J. (1976). Community metal health in a pluralistic society. *International Journal of Mental Health, 5*(2), 5-16.

Green, J. W. (1982). *Cultural awareness in the human services*. Englewood Cliffs, NJ: Prentice-Hall.

Greenwood, E. (1957). Attributes of a profession. *Social Work, 3*(3), 45-55.

Janeway, A. (1977). Beyond experience: The experiential approach to cross-cultural education. In D. Batchelder & E. G. Warner (Eds.), *Beyond experience* (pp. 5-11). Brattleboro, VT: Experiment Press.

Kroeber, A. L., & Parsons, T. (1958). The concepts of culture and of social system. *American Sociological Review, 23,* 582-583.

Marsella, A. J., & Pedersen, P. B. (Eds.). (1981). *Cross-cultural counseling and psychotherapy*. New York: Pergamon Press.

McGoldrick, M., Pearce, J. K., & Giordano, J. (Eds.). (1982). *Ethnicity and family therapy*. New York: Guilford Press.

Montalvo, B., & Gutierrez, M. (1983). A perspective for the use of the cultural dimension in family therapy. In C. J. Falicov & J. C. Hansen (Eds.), *Cultural perspectives in family therapy* (pp. 15-32). Rockville, MD: Aspen Systems Corporation.

Pedersen, P. (1983). Intercultural training of mental health providers. In D. Landis & R. W. Brislin (Eds.), *Handbook of intercultural training*. New York: Pergamon Press.

Pinderhughes, E. B. (1979). Teaching empathy in cross-cultural social work. *Social Work, 24,* 312-316.

Seelye, N. (1985). *Teaching culture: Strategies for intercultural communication*. Lincolnwood, IL: National Textbook Company.

Singer, M. R. (1987). *Intercultural communication: A perceptual approach*. Englewood Cliffs, NJ: Prentice-Hall.

Spiegel, J. (1982). An ecological model of ethnic families. In M. McGoldrick, J. K. Pearce, & J. Giordano (Eds.), *Ethnicity and family therapy* (pp. 31-51). New York: Guilford Press.

Spradley, J. P. (1979). *The ethnographic interview.* New York: Holt, Rinehart and Winston.

Sue, D. W. (1981). *Counseling the culturally different: Theory and practice.* New York: John Wiley and Sons.

Chapter 2

The Effects of Cultural Assumptions on Cross-Cultural Communication
Orlando L. Taylor

Every person involved in a counseling situation—the professional and the client—comes to that moment with a set of cultural assumptions. These assumptions, which have little to do with race, nationality, language, or socioeconomic status, are based on the rules which govern the world view and mode of behavior of that person's primary cultural group.

For purposes of this paper, culture is defined as the set of perceptions, technologies, and survival systems used by members of a group to ensure the acquisition and perpetuation of what they consider to be a high quality of life. Culture then is arbitrary and changeable. Cultures overlap and have internal variations. And cultural assumptions are learned and exist at different levels of conscious awareness.

In addition to such variables as perceptions, values, attitudes, and beliefs, culture is generally manifested in a variety of rules and modes of conduct. Failure to understand the cultural assumptions of a particular client may adversely affect therapist-client communications and overall service delivery. Areas of cultural diversity to which therapists should be sensitive include the following:

o   Family structure
o   Important events in the life cycle
o   Roles of individual members
o   Rules of interpersonal interactions
o   Communication and linguistic rules
o   Rules of decorum and discipline
o   Religious beliefs
o   Standards for health and hygiene
o   Food preferences
o   Dress and personal appearance
o   History and traditions
o   Holidays and celebrations
o   Education and teaching methods
o   Perceptions of work and play
o   Perceptions of time and space
o   Explanations of natural phenomena
o   Attitudes towards pets and animals

o   Artistic and musical values and tastes
o   Life expectations and aspirations

In order to perform effectively, clinicians must understand both their own cultural assumptions and those of the major cultural groups with which they come into contact. One can begin to understand the dynamics of one's own culture by answering questions of the type outlined in Table 1.

Cultural assumptions also include rules of both verbal and nonverbal behavior. These include the set of codified behaviors that individuals use to express their ideas, feelings, needs, values, and perceptions. Verbal rules include the phonological, semantic, grammatical, pragmatic, and discourse rules of oral communication which give rise to the particular language or dialect spoken by a person. Nonverbal rules govern eye contact, body movements, spatial relationships, touch, perceptions of time, and meanings attributed to objects.

During clinical interactions, both the clinician and the client utilize their cultural assumptions in their verbal and nonverbal communication. These exchanges are governed by a myriad of conversational and discourse rules in such areas as the following:

o   opening and closing conversations
o   taking turns during conversations
o   interrupting
o   using silence as a communicative device
o   assessing what topics of conversation are acceptable
o   using humor
o   using nonverbal conversational cues
o   laughing as a communicative device
o   determining how long and how often to speak
o   ordering of events during discourse
o   talking about illness generally and mental illness in particular

Differences in cultural assumptions, rules of verbal and nonverbal communication, and rules for interactions may disrupt the quality of communication between clinician and client and, in group clinical sessions, among the clients themselves. More specifically, such cultural differences can lead to misunderstandings, misinterpretations, and even unintentional social insults. Any of these results can seriously distort the quality of clinical data (Taylor & Payne, 1983; Wolfram, 1976), the interpretations of these data, the social climate of clinical service delivery, and ultimately, a client's desire to continue the service (or the clinician's desire to provide service).

In recent decades, a literature has emerged which could prove invaluable in preventing or reducing the occurrence of intercultural communicative disruptions during clinical encounters (see, for example, Bauman, 1972; Hymes, 1962; Kochman, 1981; and Saville-Troike, 1982, 1986).

Table 1

Some Questions to Help Identify Cultural Assumptions

Family Structure
Who is considered a member of the family?
What are the rights, roles, and responsibilities of each person?

Interpersonal Relationships
How do people greet each other?
Who may disagree with whom?
How are insults expressed?

Decorum and Discipline
How do people behave at home, in public?
What means of discipline are used?
Who has authority over whom?

Food
What is eaten, in what order, how often?
What foods are favorites, taboo, typical?
What are the rules for table manners, offering foods, handling foods, discarding foods?

Holidays and Celebrations
What holidays are observed, and what are their purposes?
Which holidays are important for children?
What cultural values are instilled in children during the holidays?

Values
What personal attributes are considered desirable? Undesirable?
What things (attributes) in the world are considered desirable? Undesirable?

Analysis of Cultural Tendencies

The theoretical constructs and analytical procedures used in the relatively new discipline known as the ethnography of communication provide the basis for addressing cross-cultural communication issues in mental health service delivery. The basic orientation of this branch of ethnography is to recognize patterns of communicative behavior as an aspect of a group's culture. Thus, language is seen "as a socially situated cultural form," the study of which must be in the context of "how language actually functions in the lives of individuals and cultural groups" (Saville-Troike, 1986, p. 55).

Saville-Troike (1986) writes:

> The subject matter of the ethnography of communication is best illustrated by one of its most general questions. What does a speaker need to know to communicate appropriately within a particular speech community, and how does he or she acquire this knowledge? Such knowledge, together with whatever skills are needed to make use of it, is termed communicative competence (Hymes, 1966). The requisite knowledge includes not only rules for communication (both linguistic and sociolinguistic) and shared rules for interaction, but also the cultural rules and knowledge that are the basis for the context and content of communicative events and interaction processes (p. 56).

From existing research in the ethnography of communication, one can derive a set of behavioral tendencies of many of the cultural groups that might be seen in various clinical situations. For example, differing cultural tendencies have been described by Payne (1986) for American Blacks, Latinos, Asians, and Anglo-Saxon whites. These cultural tendencies are generally descriptive of the indigenous traditional cultures, although they may be modified or absent in a given member of a cultural group because of education, individual preference, or acculturation toward the dominant culture. Moreover, persons from a given cultural group may exhibit few cultural tendencies from their indigenous cultural groups in public settings, choosing instead to exhibit behavior of some other cultural group (usually the dominant one).

Examples of some of the more common cultural and communicative tendencies reported for the aforementioned groups are presented in Table 2. This list can be evaluated and revised, as necessary, based on one's own ethnographic observations, personal knowledge, or understanding of the literature. Failure to recognize cultural and communicative tendencies such as those cited here, as well as their internal variations within a particular group and the tendency for "culture switching" by some members of cultural subgroups, can lead to miscommunications and poor service delivery in clinical situations.

Table 2

Some Cultural and Communicative Tendencies of Four American Subgroups

Hispanics
1. Unity and interdependence among members of the (extended) family
2. Expectation for the family and extended family to care for the young and elderly
3. Flexible sense of time
4. Physical closeness and touching during conversation
5. Emotional intensity and expression during conversation
6. Respect for tradition and traditional family and social roles
7. Preference for field-independent (social oriented) learning style

Asian Americans
1. Strong family connections
2. Respect for patience, owing to respect for history
3. Preference towards modesty, reserve, and control
4. Respect for silence
5. Low regard for argumentation
6. Respect for authority
7. Orientation toward tradition
8. Disrespect for aggression and aggressive behavior
9. Orientation towards privacy
10. Hesitancy towards spontaneity
11. Highly structured society, with lots of "do's" and "don'ts"
12. Dropping of eyes to show respect
13. Use of laughter when embarrassed
14. Taking offense at use of nicknames or use of first name only
15. Disdain for public reprimand

Blacks
1. Unity of reality and history
2. "We" vs. "I" world view
3. Preference for call/response communicative style
4. Strong "in group" tendencies resulting in perceptions of insult when outsiders use "in group" rules without authorization
5. Preference for "stylized" vs. "regimented" behavior
6. Averting of eyes during listening, direct eye contact during speaking
7. Preference for topic-associating discourse strategy
8. Preference for field-dependent (social oriented) learning style
9. Emotional intensity and expression during conversation

Anglo-Saxon Americans
1. Preference for nuclear vs. extended family
2. Respect for directness and politeness in conversation
3. Respect for traditional behaviors
4. Preference for "I" vs. "we" world view
5. Respect for individualism and competitiveness
6. High regard for "standard English"
7. Preference for promptness
8. Respect for linear vs. circular logic
9. Preference to not show emotion
10. Preference for order and control
11. Low regard for cultural explanations of life events

Table 3

Some Possible Verbal and Nonverbal Sources of Miscommunication Between Cultural Groups

Blacks
1. Touching of one's hair by another person is often considered as offensive.
2. Preference is for indirect eye contact during listening, direct eye contact during speaking as signs of attentiveness and respect.
3. Public behavior may be emotionally intense, dynamic, and demonstrative.

4. A clear distinction is made between "arguing" and "fighting." Verbal abuse is not necessarily a precursor to violence.
5. Asking "personal questions" of someone one has met for the first time is seen as improper and intrusive.
6. Interruption during conversation is usually tolerated. Competition for the floor is granted to the person who is most assertive.
7. Conversations are regarded as private between the recognized participants. "Butting in" is seen as eavesdropping and is not tolerated.
8. Use of expression "you people" is seen as pejorative and racist.

Whites (Anglo-Saxon)
Touching of one's hair by another person is a sign of affection.
Preference is for direct eye contact during listening and indirect eye contact during speaking as signs of attention and respect.
Public behavior is expected to be modest and emotionally restrained. Emotional displays are seen as irresponsible or in bad taste.
Heated arguments are viewed as suggesting that violence is imminent.

Inquiring about jobs, family, etc., of someone one has met for the first time is seen as friendly.

Rules of turn-taking in conversation dictate that one person at a time has the floor until all one's points are made.
Adding points of information or insights to a conversation in which one is not engaged is seen as being helpful.
Use of expression "you people" is tolerated.

Hispanics
1. Hissing to gain attention may be acceptable.

2. Touching is often observed between two people in conversation.
3. Avoidance of direct eye contact is sometimes a sign of attentiveness and respect; sustained direct eye contact may be interpreted as a challenge to authority.
4. Relative distance between two speakers in conversation is closer.
5. Official or business conversations are preceded by lengthy greetings, pleasantries, and other talk unrelated to the point of business.

Whites (Anglo-Saxon)
Hissing is usually considered impolite and indicates contempt.
Touching is usually unacceptable and may carry sexual overtones.
Direct eye contact is a sign of attentiveness and respect.

Relative distance between two speakers in conversation is farther apart.
Getting to the point quickly is valued.

Asians/Vietnamese
1. Touching or hand-holding between males may be acceptable.
2. Hand-holding/hugging/kissing between men and women is unacceptable.
3. A slap on the back is insulting.
4. It is not customary to shake hands with persons of the opposite sex.

Whites (Anglo-Saxons)
Touching or hand-holding between males is unacceptable.
Hand-holding/hugging/kissing between men and women in public is acceptable.
A slap on the back denotes friendliness.
It is customary to shake hands with persons of the opposite sex.

Examples of Breakdowns in Intercultural Communication

There are several interesting books which address different cultural rules for engaging in conversations across cultural lines. Although overgeneralized and somewhat stereotyped, Kochman's (1981) book on Black-white differences in communicative behaviors provides a good framework for beginning to understand how different cultural groups engage in various types of communication. Some of the verbal and nonverbal communicative behaviors which can lead to inter-ethnic conflicts among various cultural groups are presented in Table 3. These concepts are based on Kochman's work and are drawn from anecdotal observations. (The reader should be cautioned that any materials which tend to simplify in order to provide a framework for understanding are, at best, mere simplifications to be verified or challenged on a case-by-case basis.)

The following are three examples from the literature which illustrate how cultural assumptions concerning communication can interfere with the collection of valid clinical data.

Example 1

Language Elicitation from Arizona Navajo Children
(from Saville-Troike, 1986, pp. 50-51)

When I first started collecting data for research on the language of Navajo children, I, too, received no response when attempts were made to interview children. Assuming my attempts to speak Navajo were incomprehensible to the children, I asked a Navajo friend to correct my grammar and pronunciation. Instead, the entire communicative approach was corrected. When I sat by a child silently for an appropriate period of time before asking questions, fluent and willing responses were then obtained. . . .

When the first question that teachers ask a child or parent is, "What is your name?" they create an additional dimension of cultural conflict. Traditional Navajos do not believe in saying their own name, and the teacher is asking the person to violate a sociolinguistic constraint at best, and at worst a religious taboo. Navajo children (and most adults) do not tell non-Navajos when they are violating acceptable practices.

The standard box of eight color crayons presents another hurdle in the classroom. Perception of experience, including the color spectrum, is categorized differently in different languages. The "blue" and "green" crayons are placed in a single category, labelled *dotl'izh,* whereas English black corresponds to two distinct Navajo colors. . . .

The symbolic significance attached to colors may differ also. Whereas Anglo culture attributes primarily psychoaesthetic values to color (yellow is "cheerful," black is "depressing," white represents "purity," etc.), the significance and evaluation of colors in Navajo is radically different. Colors are often associated with the cardinal directions in sandpaintings and songs, the more frequent association being the following:

white:	east
yellow:	west
black:	north
blue/green:	south

Example 2

Alaskan Indian Child's Interpretation of Traditional Anglo Reading Materials
(from Salisbury, 1967)

He/she is taught to read the Dick and Jane series. Many things are confusing him: Dick and Jane are two gussuk children who play together. Yet he/she knows that boys and girls do not play together and do not share toys. They have a dog named Spot who comes indoors and does not work. Dick and Jane have a father who leaves for some mysterious place called "office" each day and never brings any food home with him. He drives a machine called an automobile on a hard-covered road called a street which has a policeman on each corner. These policemen always smile, wear funny clothing and spend their time helping children to cross the street. Why do these children need this help? Dick and Jane's mother spends a lot of time in the kitchen cooking a strange food called "cookies" on a stove which has no flame in it.

But the most bewildering part is yet to come. One day they drive out to the country which is a place where Dick and Jane's grandparents are kept. They do not live with the family and they are so glad to see Dick and Jane that it appears that they have been ostracized from the rest of the family for some terrible reason. The old people live on something called a "farm," which is a place where many strange animals are kept—a peculiar beast called a "cow," some odd looking birds called "chickens" and a "horse" which looks like a deformed moose.

Example 3

**Analysis of Traditional Navajo Values and Beliefs
Compared to Those in Mainstream Children's Books**
(from Evard & Mitchell, 1966)

Middle-class, urban values	**Traditional Navajo values**
Pets have humanlike personalities.	Pets are distinct from human personality.
Life is pictured as child-centered.	Life is adult-centered.
Adults participate in children's activities.	Children participate in adult's activities.
Germ-theory is implicitly expressed.	Good health results from harmony with nature.
Children and parents are masters of their environment.	Children accept their environment and live with it.
Children are energetic, out-going, obviously happy.	Children are passive and unexpressive.
Life is easy, safe, and bland.	Life is hard and dangerous.

Conclusion

This paper examines the communicative considerations which undergird the ethnological dimension of clinical practice. It also presents examples of some of the specific sources of culture-based communicative conflicts which might interfere with effective delivery of mental health services.

In order to integrate cross-cultural considerations into the clinical process, the clinician is encouraged to:

1. View each clinical encounter as a socially situated communicative event which is subject to the cultural rules governing such events by both the clinician and the client.
2. Recognize that clients may perform differentially under differing clinical conditions because of their cultural and language backgrounds.
3. Recognize that different modes, channels, and functions of communicative events in which individuals are expected to participate in a clinical setting may result in differing levels of linguistic or communicative performance.
4. Utilize ethnographic techniques for evaluating communicative behavior and establish cultural norms for determining the presence or absence of pathology.

5. Recognize possible sources of conflicts in cultural assumptions and communicative norms in clients prior to clinical encounters, and take steps to prevent them from occurring during service delivery.
6. Recognize that learning about culture is an ongoing process which should result in a constant reassessment and revision of ideas and greater sensitivity to cultural diversity.

References

Bauman, R. (1972). Ethnographic framework for investigation of communicative behaviors. In R. Abrahams & R. Troike (Eds.), *Language and cultural diversity in American education.* Englewood Cliffs, NJ: Prentice-Hall.

Evard, E., & Mitchell, G. C. (1966). Sally, Dick and Jane at Lukachukai. *Journal of American Indian Education, 5,* 5.

Hymes, D. (1962). The ethnography of speaking. In T. Gladwin & W. C. Sturtevant (Eds.), *Anthropology and human behavior.* Washington, DC: Anthropological Society of Washington, DC.

Hymes, D. (1966). *On communicative competence.* Paper presented at the Research Planning Conference on Language Development Among Disadvantaged Children, Yeshiva University, New York.

Kochman, T. (1981). *Black and white: Styles in conflict.* Chicago: University of Chicago Press.

Payne, K. (1986). Cultural and linguistic groups in the United States. In O. L. Taylor (Ed.), *Nature of communication disorders in culturally and linguistically diverse populations.* San Diego, CA: College-Hill Press.

Salisbury, L. H. (1967). Teaching English to Alaska natives. *Journal of American Indian Education, 6,* 4-5.

Saville-Troike, M. (1982). *The ethnography of communication.* Baltimore: University Park Press.

Saville-Troike, M. (1986). Anthropological considerations in the study of communication. In O. L. Taylor (Ed.), *Nature of communication disorders in linguistically and culturally diverse populations.* San Diego, CA: College-Hill Press.

Taylor, O. L., & Payne, K. T. (1983). Culturally valid testing: A proactive approach. *Topics in Language Disorders, 3,* 8-20.

Wolfram, W. (1976). Levels of sociolinguistic bias in testing. In D.S. Harrison & T. Trabasso (Eds.), *Seminar in Black English.* Hillsdale, NJ: Erbaum.

Part Two

Cross-Cultural Counseling

Chapter 3

Culturally Relevant Issues and Treatment Implications for Hispanics
Lillian Comas-Díaz

The Hispanic population in the United States is diverse and heterogeneous. It forms a multicultural, multiracial, and multiethnic mosaic of approximately 17 million people. Some Hispanics have recently immigrated, while the families of others have lived here since long before the arrival of the Pilgrims. The term *Hispanic,* as used by the U.S. Bureau of the Census, encompasses both persons of Spanish origin or descent and those who designate themselves as *Mexican, Mexican American, Chicano, Puerto Rican, Boricua, Cuban,* or *Other Spanish/Hispanic* (Hispanics, 1984).

Some Hispanics refer to themselves as Latinos, thereby stressing their Latin American background. Nevertheless, their attachment to the Hispanic culture and Spanish language is strong. Yet while Hispanics share a common bond of cultural background, language, and in most instances religion, the various Hispanic groups have distinct profiles. Each group has its own perceptions of itself, of other Hispanic/Latino groups, of its place in the United States, and of its country of origin (if applicable).

The diversity among Hispanics is further evidenced in demographic variables such as geographical distribution, urban-rural dwelling, level of acculturation, national origin (Mexican, Puerto Rican, Cuban), socioeconomic class, gender, and age. Of these, socioeconomic class represents a particularly powerful variable—often differences in behavior that are attributed to cultural differences really reflect socioeconomic differences. Moreover, diversity among Hispanics is mediated by their generational status, language preference, and political status (immigrant or native). Immigrants can be further divided into those that are documented and those that are not (i.e., illegal aliens). Another important subgroup consists of Hispanics who have experienced political repression and civil war trauma in their own countries. Many of these political refugees and displaced individuals clearly require specialized mental health services (Vargas, 1984). Elsewhere in this volume, García and Rodríguez discuss the psychological consequences of political repression among Central American and Argentinian individuals.

The purpose of this chapter is to discuss the ethnocultural values of Hispanics and their implications for mental health treatment. Discussing the mental health needs of this heterogeneous population poses a challenge.

31

Nevertheless, their common cultural background causes Hispanics to be sufficiently distinct from non-Hispanics to warrant a differential analysis of their mental health needs. Notwithstanding Hispanic diversity, the author will concentrate on this group's similarities. Based on her clinical experience with Hispanics from different backgrounds, she is convinced that these characteristics are grounded on their common cultural bond.

Hispanic Cultural Values

The role of culture as a determinant of health and illness behaviors has been pointed out elsewhere (Harwood, 1981). For Hispanics, as with any other ethnic group, the cultural context is a crucial consideration for the effective delivery of mental health services. Thus, understanding Hispanic cultural values, family dynamics, and health beliefs and practices, as well as the process of acculturation, increases a clinician's effectiveness.

Family Dynamics

Much has been written about Hispanic families in the mental health literature (Bernal, 1982; Falicov, 1982; García-Preto, 1982). The traditional Hispanic family tends to be an extended one, where members beyond the nuclear unit—such as grandparents, aunts, uncles, cousins, and others—are considered integral to the concept of family. This cultural norm is reinforced by the value of *familismo* (familism). Defined as the tendency to extend kinship relationship beyond the nuclear family boundaries, *familismo* emphasizes interdependence over independence, affiliation over confrontation, and cooperation over competition (Falicov, 1982). Hispanic families are further extended to include non-blood-related individuals such as close family friends, who are often called "uncle" or "aunt" and treated accordingly.

Many Hispanic clients perceive their therapist as part of their extended kinship network. This tendency can initially help with the development of the therapeutic alliance. As a member of the family, the clinician has more acceptance, influence, and impact within the family network. Although this may facilitate a patient's engagement into treatment, it can also interfere with the therapeutic process if transference and countertransference are not monitored carefully.

Hispanics attribute primordial importance to the collective. That is, the needs of the family have priority over the needs of the individual. The interdependence prevalent among many Hispanic families reinforces the value of the collective. Similarly, activities surrounding family developmental milestones take on a high priority, and all family members are expected to participate. Families expect to be together at events such as weddings, baptisms, special anniversaries, and funerals, as well as for the celebration of holidays. Participation in such family rituals reinforces and cements the sense of belonging to the group. This is particularly relevant for Hispanic patients who do not reside with their extended families.

The sense of family is so vital for the Hispanic patient that Canino and Canino (1982) have argued that mental illness among Hispanics is a family affair and not an individual situation. Consequently, they recommend family involvement in treatment. Involving family members in some of the treatment states (for example, evaluation, crisis situations, and termination) can indeed be very beneficial. Furthermore, I have found that conducting family genograms is useful even while working in individual psychotherapy. In addition to the usual information obtained through the use of genograms, it is important to identify the patient's namesake. Many Hispanics are named after family members, and identifying such members and understanding their "histories" may help reveal the patient's conflicts. There is usually an identification (attributed by the family, the patient, or both) between the patient and his or her namesake. This tendency is so strong in Latin America that Gabriel García Márquez's (1969) Nobel Prize-winning novel, *One Hundred Years of Solitude*, is based on the characters' telling of the histories of the relatives for whom they were named.

Another traditional cultural value stressing the emphasis on the collective is the system of *compadrazgo* (co-parenting). This extended family system is based on the relationship resulting from child baptism. The baptismal *compadres* (co-parents) become the child's *padrinos* (godparents) and, as such, the surrogate parents. *Compadres* are traditionally consulted during periods of stress, illness, or other problems, and are thus involved in the family decision-making process. *Compadrazgo* stipulates that the baptismal godparents are responsible for the child's welfare if the biological parents die. Although this traditional value may no longer be operative, Hispanics still have the tendency to seek out surrogate parents for their children. Thus *compadrazgo* is closely related to the value of familism.

Another cultural value ingrained in the traditional Hispanic family is *respeto* (respect). This concept governs all positive reciprocal interpersonal relationships, dictating the appropriate deferential behavior toward others on the basis of age, socioeconomic position, sex, and authority status. Thus older people deserve respect from younger people, men from women, parents from offspring, employers from employees, and so on. By virtue of their therapeutic function, clinicians are perceived as authority figures and, as such, are awarded *respeto*. They are considered experts due to their training and education.

Hispanic adult patients likewise expect clinicians to treat them with *respeto*. To achieve this, the clinician should address them in a formal manner using *Señor* (Mr.), *Señora* (Mrs.), or *Señorita* (Miss) with their last names. This mode of address should be observed, at least initially, although later on patients can be asked what they prefer to be called. This attitude of respect is particularly relevant for the younger clinician/older patient dyad. Perceived disrespect from the therapist may result in premature treatment termination.

Sex Roles

In the traditional Hispanic culture, gender roles are rigidly defined. Nevertheless, male/female relationships among Hispanics tend to be complex and paradoxical. Traditionally, the Hispanic family is patriarchal, with an authoritarian father and a submissive mother (Falicov, 1982). Boys and girls are taught two very different codes of sexual behavior. Whereas Hispanic women are traditionally expected to be sentimental, gentle, intuitive, impulsive, docile, submissive, dependent, and timid, the men are expected to be cold, intellectual, rational, profound, strong, authoritarian, independent, and brave (Senour, 1977). This rigid demarcation of sex roles encourages a double moral standard for the sexes, exemplified in the *marianismo/machismo* syndrome.

Machismo literally means maleness or virility, but culturally it means that the man is the provider and is responsible for the welfare, honor, dignity, and protection of the family. In its extreme form, *machismo* is manifested through physical dominance of women and excessive alcohol consumption (Giraldo, 1972). Furthermore, *machismo* dictates that the Hispanic male must constantly signal his sexual availability; seductive behavior is mandatory regardless of marital status (Sluzki, 1982). Paradoxically, the *macho* must protect his female relatives from the sexual advances of other men while making as many sexual conquests as possible himself. Although *machismo* may be more prevalent among lower socioeconomic classes (Kinzer, 1973), it nevertheless influences behavior in all strata of Hispanic/Latino society (Giraldo, 1972).

From a psychodynamic perspective, Aramoni (1982) argues that *machismo* can be perceived as men's effort to compensate for their everpresent, powerfully demanding, and suffering mothers, as well as to identify with their psychologically absent fathers. More recently, *machismo* has been examined from a socioeconomic and historical perspective, which emphasizes more the male's role as provider and supporter, and its contradictory, adaptive, regressive, and dynamic features (De La Cancela, 1986).

The counterpart of *machismo* for women is *marianismo*, a concept based on the Catholic worship of the Mother Mary, who is seen as both a virgin and a madonna. *Marianismo* predicates that women are spiritually superior to men, and therefore capable of enduring all suffering inflicted by men (Stevens, 1973). Accordingly, unmarried women are expected to be chaste and virginal and not to demonstrate interest in sex once they are married. When they become mothers, Hispanic women attain the status of *madonnas* and are expected to sacrifice in favor of their children and husbands. In noting the high incidence of somatic complaints among low-income Hispanic women who are in psychotherapy, Espin (1985) suggests that these complaints may well be a reaction to the self-sacrifice dictum, especially since somatization is a culturally accepted mode of expressing needs and anxieties.

The *marianista* code rewards women who adhere to it (Stevens, 1973). Because motherhood is sacred, women who bear children enjoy a certain degree of power despite their outward submissiveness. Conversely, women who do not conform to the code risk social censorship. As a consequence, a dichotomous classification of women is reinforced (i.e., the Madonna/whore complex). Some Hispanic females may present to therapy struggling with issues of sexuality based on these contradictory connotations concerning sexual activity.

Another sex role characteristic of some Hispanic women is *hembrismo*, which literally means femaleness. *Hembrismo* has been described as a cultural revenge to *machismo* (Habach, 1972) and as a frustrated attempt to imitate a male, occurring in a sociosexual spectrum of idealized roles (Gomez, 1982). *Hembrismo* is a natural reaction within a historical context and shares common elements with the women's movement in the areas of social and political goals (Gomez, 1982). *Hembrismo* connotes strength, perseverance, flexibility, and an ability for survival. However, it can also translate into the woman's attempt to fulfill her multiple role expectations as a mother, wife, worker, daughter, and member of the community—in other words, the superwomen working the *doble jornada* (or double day—i.e., working both at home and outside the home). This situation can generate stress and emotional problems for the woman behaving in the *hembrista* fashion. Likewise, many Hispanic women may present to treatment with symptoms of *marianista* behavior at home and *hembrista* behavior at work.

Traditional sex roles are undergoing change among Hispanics in the United States. For one thing, the Hispanic traditional culture, including its *machismo/marianismo* aspects, is not reinforced by the mainstream American culture. Furthermore, cultural transition itself often encourages a sexual role reversal for Hispanic men and women. The pressures of economic survival in this country, as well as the type of skills that are marketable, have caused a role reversal among many low-income Hispanic immigrants since it is often easier for the women to obtain employment in the United States by selling their sewing and domestic skills than it is for the men.

Such role reversal can create marital and family problems. However, cultural transition tends to give individuals a certain plasticity, particularly within their gender roles. Despite the apparent rigidity of Hispanic sex roles, there is flexibility which allows for change. In this author's clinical experience with Hispanic couples, she has found that challenging traditional dysfunctional sex roles is easier to accomplish with couples who are working on coping with cultural differences than with those who remain in a culturally homogeneous environment. Furthermore, the value of *hembrismo* can provide an archetype for changing sex roles.

The appearance of the power distribution between Hispanic males and females can be deceiving. In a study of sex roles among Hispanics in the United States, Canino (1982) found that on the surface, both husband and wife espoused traditional attitudes. However, when couples were interviewed more extensively and were observed during actual decision making, most of the couples shared the decision-making process. Most of the couples studied by Canino were Puerto Ricans, but her findings seem relevant to other Hispanic populations as well. Among Mexican American couples, sex role stereotyping as it affects the decision-making process is also deceiving. Falicov (1982) reports that while in some Mexican American families the husbands are domineering and patriarchal, others are submissive and depend upon their wives to make major decisions, while still other families have an egalitarian power structure These research findings and clinical observations suggest that the cultural context needs to be considered when working with Hispanic couples and families.

Gender Issues and the Clinician/Patient Relationship

The clinician working with Hispanics needs to be attentive to gender role issues and recognize that the clear-cut demarcations between the sexes in traditional Hispanic culture may affect therapist-patient relations. Hispanic patients will tend to have different expectations depending on the gender of their clinicians. Because Hispanic women are generally expected to attend to the family's health needs and are attributed with the role of healers, female clinicians may be seen as conforming to this cultural expectation. Nevertheless, Hispanic males frequently feel uncomfortable discussing their sexual concerns with female therapists (Padilla, 1981). Instead, they prefer to discuss *machismo*-related issues with a male clinician (De La Cancela, 1986). Conversely, most Hispanic women prefer to discuss their personal problems with a female therapist (Hynes & Werbin, 1977).

Because of the strength of familism, therapy tends to elicit a stronger than usual transference reaction among Hispanic patients. Male clinicians come to represent a father figure, while female clinicians are perceived as representing a nurturing and caring figure. For male therapists, the negative aspect of such cultural transference involves being perceived as authoritarian, distant, and controlling, thus hindering the development of a working therapeutic alliance. For females, the danger rests on the attribution of "martyrdom" to the therapist, thus compromising the patient's acceptance of responsibility and his or her ability to actively work in treatment.

Maldonado-Sierra and Trent (1960) explored some of these issues in a group psychotherapy format with schizophrenics. Based on the Latin American cultural values, the authors argued that family dynamics induced unconscious resentment toward male authority figures due to the dominant and authoritarian role that the father traditionally exercises. They found that young people faced with personal problems tended to relate in a more confidential manner with an older sibling or peer than with paternal figures. Thus, the authors introduced a sibling figure, in the form of a psychiatric resident, to a treatment team composed of an older male psychiatrist and a female social worker. The authors found the sibling relationship to be a highly valuable feature in the treatment format. These clinical observations suggest that clinicians need to be aware of the possibility of transference stemming from these cultural dynamics, and may want to add a facilitative peer or sibling-oriented character to the therapeutic relationship.

Interpersonal and Communication Styles

The interpersonal and communication styles of Hispanics tend to differ from those of non-Hispanic populations in culturally distinctive ways. *Personalismo* is the tendency to prefer personal contacts over impersonal or institutional ones. Hispanics tend to rely more on their own personal estimation of a person rather than on the person's economic position or material achievements. This style of interaction, while personal, is not informal. *Personalismo* is reflected in the tendency of Hispanic patients to relate to their therapist personally rather than relate to an institution or clinic which is perceived as impersonal. Thus they tend to develop a strong personal relationship with their therapist, regardless of institutional affiliation. If their therapist leaves, they may stop treatment rather than see another therapist. Consequently, when transferring patients to another therapist, it is usually helpful if the outgoing therapist personally introduces the new clinician to the patient. Developing a relationship between the new therapist and patient before the previous therapist leaves, and using the previous therapist to cement the new relationship, can prove very beneficial.

Both *personalismo* and *familismo* encourage Hispanic patients to perceive the therapist as a member of the family. While this can facilitate a patient's engagement into therapy, it can also place unrealistic demands on the clinician. For example, it is not uncommon for Hispanic patients to invite their therapist to family celebrations such as birthdays, weddings, and funerals. Although these invitations may be in line with their cultural values, they can also result in attempts to resist treatment by placing the therapist in a position of a friend rather than mental health professional. Moreover, a clinician who decides to attend these types of events may become swamped with invitations, all of which must be accepted so as not to cause feelings of rejection. The author personally declines such invitations diplomatically, unless the treatment is being terminated and attendance at the event can be placed within this context. Therapists must of course use their own clinical judgment, examining the consequences of their actions while dealing with these types of situations.

Another related value that governs interpersonal relations among Hispanics is *confianza* (which can be loosely translated as trust that requires a long time to develop). Personal relations are based on *confianza*. The therapeutic relationship, although a formal one, deals with intimate personal issues, and as such, requires the presence of *confianza*. Therapist-patient relationships tend to work better when sufficient *confianza* has developed. In fact, in the absence of *confianza*, sexual issues will not be discussed. Although most Hispanic patients immediately attribute authority and respect to the therapist, he or she needs to develop and gain *confianza* in order to be effective.

Verbal communication among Hispanics tends to be formal, guided by cultural values such as *respeto*, courtesy, and *personalismo*. Additionally, verbal communication is guided by *simpatía*. This cultural value places emphasis on maintaining a pleasant demeanor, in order to reduce conflict and promote agreement. Within the therapeutic situation, a patient's *simpatía* may lead to unassertiveness and indirect expression of feelings. Patients may avoid confrontation and conflict by not disagreeing with the clinician or by not expressing doubts and concerns about their treatment.

As an authority figure, the therapist is perceived as having the responsibility for clarifying issues surrounding treatment. Notwithstanding the cultural expectation of *simpatía,* the therapist can teach the patient assertiveness techniques to facilitate the direct expression of negative feelings. The caveat here, however, is to offer the training in a culturally relevant manner. The interested reader is advised to review the assertiveness training developed by Comas-Díaz and Duncan (1985), which takes into consideration the cultural context.

While their verbal expression tends to be circumscribed, Hispanics communicate expansively in nonverbal ways. Body language achieves a pivotal importance, but clinicians need to be aware of the subtleties of nonverbal communication since there are cultural differences in body language. For example, the appropriate distance for social interaction between Hispanics is less than the two feet or more that Anglos consider appropriate (Hall, 1969). Furthermore, Hispanics are used to more frequent touching than Anglos; thus clinicians may want to shake hands with their patients while greeting them. Likewise, clinicians need to be conscious of their own nonverbal communication. Hispanics tend to be very adept at interpreting a speaker's body language. This is particularly relevant for English-limited individuals who will rely even more on nonverbal cues (Comas-Díaz, Thorngren, Roy, Rudner, & Cook, 1988).

Religion and Folk Beliefs

Religion, like culture, is a pervasive force in influencing the behavior of Hispanics. It not only affects their conception of mental illness and treatment, but it also influences their health-seeking behaviors. Some authors have suggested that their adherence to traditional Catholic values—particularly the religious value placed on enduring human suffering and on self-denial—prevents some Hispanics from seeking treatment (Acosta, Yamamoto, & Evans, 1982).

Although Catholicism is their predominant religion, Hispanics nonetheless are a religiously diverse population that includes Protestant, Pentecostal, Jehovah's Witness, and other evangelical and fundamentalist faiths. Regardless of their religious affiliation, Hispanics typically place a high value on spiritual matters. Churches provide support, and at times substitute for the extended family that was left behind by Hispanic immigrants. For church-going Hispanics, the priest (or pastor) is frequently a key figure in their lives. Hispanics often seek a priest's advice during major life crises, including times of illness. Thus, during critical periods religious leaders can act as auxiliary helpers in the treatment process.

Despite their religiosity, many Hispanics believe in folk healing. This is consistent with the premise that they can make contact with God and the supernatural without the intervention of the traditional church (García-Preto, 1982). Prevalent among Cubans and other Caribbeans is the concept of *santería,* which combines the African Yoruban deities with the Catholic saints (Sandoval, 1977). The *santero(a)* is both a priest(ess) and a healer who treats *bilingo*, or hex. *Espiritismo* is a belief which predicates that the world is populated with spirits, including religious figures, who intervene in the lives of individuals (Kardec, 1957). A significant number of Puerto Ricans and other Hispanics believe that *espiritistas* (spiritualists or mediums) can communicate with the spirits and have the power of healing. Specifically, spiritualists are believed able to treat the *ataque,* a seizure-like conversion syndrome characterized by mutism, violence, hyperventilation, hyperkinesis, and uncommunicativeness (Fernández-Marina, 1961).

Among some Mexican Americans and other Latinos, belief in *curanderísmo* is popular. *Curanderísmo* is a folk healing and belief system prevalent among many Latin Americans that stresses the Indian and meso-Indian heritage, utilizing prayers, messages, and herbs as treatment (Maduro, 1983). The *curandero(a)* is the healer and his or her healing abilities are perceived as "a gift from God." *Curanderísmo* treats folk illnesses such as *susto* (magical fright or soul loss) and *mal puesto* (hex) (Martinez, 1988). Another folk belief prevalent among some Hispanics is the hot and cold theory (Currier, 1966). According to Harwood (1971), this belief is based on the Hippocratic theory and the notion that the human body contains four humors or liquids: blood (hot and wet), phlegm (cold and wet), black bile (cold and dry), and yellow bile (hot and dry). Disease is caused by a humoral imbalance which foods and medications can cure by restoring the balance. Thus, a "hot" illness is cured by balancing it with "cold" medications and foods, while a "cold" illness is treated with "hot" substances.

There is some controversy as to the degree of adherence by Hispanics to folk beliefs. However, clinicians need to recognize that at times, many Hispanics, regardless of their acculturation, adhere to these beliefs. Castro, Furth, and Karlow (1984) investigated whether less acculturated Mexicans had a significantly different conceptual system of beliefs concerning health and illness than more acculturated Mexicans and Anglo women. The researchers' findings revealed that Mexican American women expressed mild acceptance of Mexican folk beliefs, a moderate acceptance of hot-cold, and a strong acceptance of biomedical beliefs (e.g., that cardiovascular stress causes illness). The less acculturated women reported a somewhat lower sense of responsibility and control over their own health, and a strong belief in hot-cold theory. According to the researchers, the findings suggest that Mexican-origin women have a dual system of belief which tends to weaken but not disappear with increasing acculturation. Some Hispanics seek the services of folk healers while simultaneously receiving professional health care. Therefore, it behooves clinicians working with Hispanic populations to be aware of the existence of these folk beliefs.

Acculturation

The concept of acculturation as it mediates mental health issues among Hispanics is receiving attention (Padilla, 1980). Acculturation is a fluid quality; thus bicultural individuals can be more Hispanic-oriented in one context and more mainstream-oriented in another context.

Several reactions to acculturation in the form of clinical typologies have been reported. Within a psychotherapeutic context, the author (Comas-Díaz, 1982) discussed three degrees of acculturation. Low in the acculturation spectrum is the Hispanic who has limited contact with mainstream American society. Typical of this category is the person who immigrates to the United States during middle age, has limited education, speaks only Spanish, and rigidly adheres to Hispanic cultural values. The second classification is characterized by high acculturation and assimilation which may result in Hispanics denying their ethnic identity. Individuals in this position may identify themselves as American, Black, Italian, or some other nationality. The third category, labeled the "cultural schizophrenic" model, consists of Hispanics with some degree of acculturation who operate within both cultures. Such persons may at times act as a cultural bridge, and at other times may be confused by conflicting values.

Under stress this person may be unable to successfully integrate the two cultures. However, when the "culturally schizophrenic" person can eventually synthesize both cultures, a new integrative cultural repertoire can be achieved.

These typologies are not exhaustive; indeed, they represent a continuum of coping styles. Another category is the "culturally amphibious" person who is able to live successfully in both the Hispanic and the American cultures (Comas-Díaz, 1988). These individuals usually can "pass" as non-Hispanics (i.e., they are light-skinned and do not speak with an accent); they are bilingual and bicultural and, like amphibian animals, can survive in two different environments without difficulties. Some remain in this amphibian state, while others may move to a different classification, depending on their developmental stage or political status. "Culturally amphibious" Hispanics differ from the "cultural schizophrenics" in that the former can choose which environment they want to live in without having others impose ethnic identifications on them. All of these typologies have implications for mental health. Thus, it is important to assess the patient's acculturation level and to address this issue in treatment.

Help-Seeking Behavior

Coping Styles

Hispanics have available in their repertoires coping styles that are congruent with their cultural backgrounds. According to Castro and his associates (1984), the concept of self-control among Mexicans and Mexican Americans is different from the one prevalent in the Anglo culture. They argue that the Mexican concept of *controlarse* includes: (a) the ability to withstand stress in times of adversity; (b) *aguantarse* (endurance), a passive resignation in which the person accepts his or her fate; (c) *resignarse* (resignation), a more active cognitive coping; and (d) *sobreponerse*, the ability to work through a problem or to overcome adversity. The author has found these coping styles to be prevalent among other Hispanic groups as well.

These coping styles directly impact upon the help-seeking behaviors of Hispanics. Individuals who embrace the *controlarse* paradigm are unlikely to seek professional mental health treatment when first facing a problem. Their help-seeking pathway tends to include family and other support systems first; only as a last resort will they turn to the professional system. Moreover, when faced with mental health problems, many Hispanics turn to medical doctors, while others resort to folk practices.

A related concept affecting the coping styles of Hispanics is cultural fatalism or the belief that some things are meant to happen regardless of the individual's intervention (*Que será, será*—What will be, will be). Cultural fatalism reflects an external locus of control in which people perceive the events that happen to them to be the result of luck, fate, or powers beyond their control rather than dependent on their own behavior (Rotter, 1966). For some Hispanics with an external locus of control, mental illness may be perceived as God's testing of the individual.

Cultural fatalism also relates to socioeconomic class and ethnic identity. Ross, Mirowsky, and Cockerham (1983) found that while persons of Mexican identity tended to have a fatalistic outlook on life, this fatalism was more pronounced among those of a lower socioeconomic class.

Expectations from Mental Health Services

The Hispanic culture does not differentiate between physical and emotional concerns (Padilla & Ruiz, 1973) in the same way the Anglo culture does. For example, Hispanics generally believe that strong emotions cause physical illness (Maduro, 1983). Therefore, they see the mental state affecting the physical condition and vice versa.

This body/mind interrelationship has helped to reinforce the stereotype that Hispanics are not psychologically minded. However, this author and associates (Comas-Díaz, Geller, Melgoza, & Baker, 1982) found that Hispanics requesting services at a community mental health clinic typically presented complaints of a psychological nature, including depression, anxiety, concentration problems, obsessions and compulsions, fears, and sleep problems. Many also cited physical and financial problems, which was consistent with their holistic approach to health and illness. When results were analyzed by sex, higher reporting of drug problems, antisocial behavior, and suicidal tendencies among Hispanic males were found. The researchers concluded that the overall findings challenge previous portrayals of Hispanics as unsuitable for intensive psychotherapy because of their tendency to define their mental health problems as somatic or medical rather than psychological in nature.

The investigation also studied the expectations of Hispanic patients regarding treatment and their therapist. Findings indicated that Hispanics expected the therapist to be decisive and to give advice, while they saw themselves as active participants with personal responsibility for the outcome of therapy. Hispanic patients showed grounding in psychological precepts in that they accepted unconscious feelings and ambivalence towards others. They also acknowledged the importance and the value of expressing their thoughts and feelings. They expressed a desire for a therapeutic relationship in which they could talk freely about themselves and their problems, their thoughts and feelings. Moreover, they reported a willingness to persist in this type of experience despite the fact that it was apt to be distressing at times.

Many Hispanic patients are steered to mental health services through the medical system. It has been stated that Mexican Americans seek out professional mental health services as a last resort, usually using other health service providers initially (Keefe, Padilla, & Carlos, 1978). However, this pattern of help-seeking behavior is equally characteristic of non-Hispanics of low socioeconomic status (Lorion, 1974), and therefore may not necessarily be an ethnic trait. In this author's experience, Hispanic patients tend to express a complex set of treatment expectations including psychological, medical, and environmental variables. It is incumbent upon the clinician to properly assess and effectively address their needs.

Use of Medications

The treatment expectations of Hispanic patients have clear implications for the dynamics and use of medications. Espousing a medical expectation of mental health treatment is congruent with expecting to receive medications or a concrete service. Discussion about these expectations is crucial for preventing premature termination of therapy. When medication is provided, however, another problem may emerge. Many patients take the medication on an "as needed" basis rather than the number of times indicated. Ramos-McKay, Comas-Díaz, and Rivera (1988) found that many Puerto Rican patients believe that taking the prescribed amount of medication can be harmful. Furthermore, some patients may initially take the prescribed medication, but if their symptoms are not immediately alleviated, they may stop their intake without consulting the clinician. On the other hand, when medication is not prescribed, the clinician should clearly explain to the patient why it is not necessary in his or her case. This will help prevent the tendency of such patients to use medications prescribed to relatives or friends, or to self-medicate.

Treatment of Hispanic Patients

A variety of treatment modalities have been used with Hispanic patients. As indicated before, some clinicians tend to make use of cultural values such as *familismo* in family therapy (Canino & Canino, 1982) and *marianismo* in all-female (Hynes & Werbin, 1977) and *machismo* in all-male (De La Cancela, 1986) group psychotherapy. Similarly, several treatment orientations have been successfully utilized including behavioral (Stumphauzer & Davis, 1983), cognitive and behavioral (Comas-Díaz, 1981), dynamically oriented (Olarte & Lenz, 1984), and feminist (Comas-Díaz, 1988) psychotherapies. In addition, culturally relevant treatment interventions such as *cuento* therapy (the use of folktales in treatment) have also been developed (Costantino, Malgady, & Rogler, 1985). There is no single method or approach that can be considered the best for treating Hispanics; some patients respond better to one approach/modality treatment and some to another, depending on their presenting complaints.

Regardless of the treatment approach/modality used with Hispanic patients, clinicians need to address the complex set of treatment expectations Hispanics have involving a multiplicity of psychological, physical, and environmental dimensions. For instance, the author gives great weight to a patient's sociocultural context. Additionally, she has found it very useful to apply behavioral approaches such as relaxation techniques and assertiveness training during the beginning phase of treatment, while maintaining a dynamic conceptualization of the therapeutic process. Similarly, Cerventes and Castro (1985) have argued for the conceptualization of a stress-mediation-outcome framework while working with Hispanic patients. They see psychological disturbances as the result of an interaction between the person, the environment, and his or her resources (both internal and external) in confronting stressful life circumstances. Hispanics' complex set of treatment expectations is congruent with this approach.

Linguistic issues are pivotal in the diagnosis and treatment of Hispanics (Marcos, Urcuyo, Kesselman, & Alpert, 1973). Although an extensive discussion of this topic is beyond the scope of this chapter, the interested reader can examine the available literature which discusses the effects of language in the treatment of bilingual Hispanic patients (Marcos, 1976; Rozensky & Gomez, 1983). The ideal situation is to have a bilingual clinician. This person can better address issues such as language switching and the usage of words that do not have a literal translation in English or Spanish. However, given the limited number of bilingual mental health professionals, many clinicians have no choice but to use trained interpreters. Acosta and Cristo (1981) describe the development and successful implementation of a bilingual interpreter program, in which interpreters are specially trained in bilingual proficiency, interpreting style, and mental health terminology. In addition, the interpreters participate in ongoing training involving supervisory and peer feedback, role playing, and viewing of audio and video tapes of actual therapist/patient interactions. The interpreters in this program also work as community aides. Bilingual/bicultural professional staff coordinate the program and act as supervisors. The authors contend that their model has significantly increased the utilization of clinics by Hispanic patients.

Identity is another major issue among Hispanics that should be examined in therapy. In their work with ethnoculturally translocated individuals, members of minority groups, and patients in cross-cultural psychotherapy, Comas-Díaz and Jacobsen (1987) introduce the ethnocultural identification process. They argue that these patients frequently experience disturbances of their ethnocultural identities, resulting in their attributing ethnocultural qualities to their therapists during therapy. Ethnocultural identification may be used to foster a therapeutic identification in which the therapist reflects pieces of the patient's conflicted ethnocultural identity. The authors state that ethnocultural identification can be utilized as an auxiliary therapeutic tool to facilitate coping with changing cultural values and transitional experiences, and to promote the integration of the ethnocultural self into a consolidated sense of identity.

Conclusion

Although the growing Hispanic population in the United States is very diverse, their common cultural background causes Hispanics to be sufficiently distinct from non-Hispanics to warrant a differential analysis of their mental health needs. Many treatment orientations and modalities have been used successfully—including behavior, cognitive, psychodynamic, and feminist approaches within individual, family, group, and couples formats. However, in order to be effective, clinicians need to understand traditional Hispanic cultural values including sex roles, the rules for interpersonal and communication style, and religious and folk beliefs, as well as the process of acculturation. Linguistic considerations and issues relating to identity also require special emphasis while working with this population. Furthermore, clinicians need to be aware of their Hispanic patients' complex set of treatment expectations and need to address them in therapy. In sum, treatment of Hispanics needs to be ethnoculturally relevant in order to be effective.

References

Acosta, F. X., & Cristo, M. H. (1981). Development of a bilingual interpreter program: An alternative model for Spanish-speaking services. *Professional Psychology, 12*(4), 474-481.

Acosta, F. X., Yamamoto, J., & Evans, L. A. (1982). *Effective psychotherapy for low–income and minority patients.* New York: Plenum Press.

Aramoni, A. (1982). Machismo. *Psychology Today, 5*(8), 69-72.

Bernal, G. (1982). Cuban families. In M. McGoldrick, J. K. Pearce, & J. Giordano (Eds.), Ethnicity and family therapy (pp. 187-207). New York: The Guilford Press.

Canino, G. (1982). Transactional family patterns: A preliminary exploration of Puerto Rican female adolescents. In R. E. Zambrana (Ed.), *Work, family and health: Latina women in transition* (pp. 27-36). New York: Hispanic Research Center, Fordham University.

Canino G., & Canino, I. A. (1982). Culturally syntonic family therapy for migrant Puerto Ricans. *Hospital and Community Psychiatry, 33*(4), 299-303.

Castro, F. G., Furth, P., & Karlow, H. (1984). The health beliefs of Mexican, Mexican American and Anglo American Women. *Hispanic Journal of Behavioral Sciences, 6*(4), 365-383.

Cervantes, R. C., & Castro, F. G. (1985). Stress, coping and Mexican American health: A systematic review. *Hispanic Journal of Behavioral Sciences, 7,* 1-73.

Comas-Díaz, L. (1981). Effects of cognitive and behavioral group treatment in the depressive symptomatology of Puerto Rican women. *Journal of Consulting and Clinical Psychology, 49*(5), 627-632.

Comas-Díaz, L. (1982). Mental health needs of mainland Puerto Rican women. In R. E. Zambrana (Ed.), *Work, family and health: Latina women in transition* (pp. 1-10). New York: Hispanic Research Center, Fordham University.

Comas-Díaz, L. (1988). Feminist therapy with Hispanic/Latina women: Myth or reality? *Women & Therapy, 6*(4), 39-61.

Comas-Díaz, L., & Duncan, J. W. (1985). The cultural context: A factor in assertiveness training with mainland Puerto Rican women. *Psychology of Women Quarterly, 9*(4), 463-475.

Comas-Díaz, L., Geller, J. D., Melgoza, B., & Baker, R. (1982, August). *Attitudes and expectations about mental health services among Hispanics and Afro-Americans.* Paper presented at the 90th Annual Meeting of the American Psychological Association, Washington, DC.

Comas-Díaz, L., & Jacobsen, F. M. (1987). Ethnocultural identification in psychotherapy. *Psychiatry, 50*(3), 232-241.

Comas-Díaz, L., Thorngren, M., Roy, I., Rudner, N., & Cook, A. T. (1988). *Delivering preventive health care to Hispanics: A manual for providers.* Washington, DC: COSSMHO.

Costantino, G., Malgady, R., & Rogler, L. H. (1985). *Cuento therapy: Folktales as a culturally sensitive psychotherapy for Hispanic children.* New York: Hispanic Research Center, Fordham University.

Currier, R. L. (1966). The hot-cold syndrome and symbolic balance in Mexican and Spanish-American folk medicine. *Ethnology, 5,* 251-263.

De La Cancela, V. (1986). A critical analysis of Puerto Rican machismo: Implications for clinical practice. *Psychotherapy, 2*(2), 291-296.

Espin, O. M. (1985). Psychotherapy with Hispanic women: Some considerations. In P. Pedersen (Ed.), *Handbook of cross-cultural counseling and therapy* (pp. 165-171). Westport, CT: Greenwood Press.

Falicov, C. J. (1982). Mexican families. In M. McGoldrick, J. K. Pearce, & J. Giordano (Eds.), *Ethnicity and family therapy* (pp. 134-163). New York: The Guilford Press.

Fernández-Marina, R. (1961). The Puerto Rican syndrome: Its dynamics and cultural determinants. *Psychiatry, 24,* 79-82.

García Márquez, G. (1969). *Cien anos de soledad* [One hundred years of solitude]. Buenos Aires: Editorial Sudamericana.

García-Preto, N. (1982). Puerto Rican families. In M. McGoldrick, J. K. Pearce, & J. Giordano (Eds.), *Ethnicity and family therapy* (pp. 164-186). New York: The Guilford Press.

Giraldo, D. (1972). El machismo como fenomeno psicocultural [Machismo as a psychocultural phenomenon]. *Revista Latino-Americana de Psicologia, 4* (3), 295-309.

Gomez, A. M. (1982). Puerto Rican American. In A. Gaw (Ed.), *Cross-cultural psychiatry* (pp. 109-136). Littleton, MA: John Wright.

Habach, E. (1972). *Ni machismo, ni hembrismo* [Neither *machismo* nor *hembrismo*]. Colección Protesta. Caracas: Publicaciones EPLA.

Hall, E. T. (1969). The silent language. In R. O'Brien (Ed.), *Readings in general sociology* (pp. 60-64). Boston: Houghton Mifflin.

Harwood, A. (1971). The hot-cold theory of disease: Implications for treatment of Puerto Rican patients. *The Journal of the American Medical Association, 216*(7), 1153-1158.

Harwood, A. (1981). *Ethnicity and medical care*. Cambridge, MA: Harvard University Press.

Hispanics: Challenges and opportunities (1984, June). New York: Ford Foundation. (Available from the Ford Foundation, Office of Reports, 320 East 43rd St., New York, N.Y. 10017)

Hynes, K., & Werbin, J. (1977). Group psychotherapy for Spanish-speaking women. *Psychiatric Annals, 7*(12), 52-63.

Kardec, A. (1957). *El libro de los espiritus* [The spirits' book]. Mexico: Editorial Diana.

Keefe, S. W., Padilla, A. M., & Carlos, M. L. (1978). *Emotional support system in two cultures: A comparison of Mexican Americans and Anglo Americans* (Occasional Paper No. 7). Los Angeles: University of California, Spanish Speaking Mental Health Research Center.

Kinzer, N. (1973). Women in Latin America: Priests, machos, and babies, or Latin American women and the Manichean heresy. *Journal of Marriage and the Family, 35,* 299-312.

Lorion, R. P. (1974). Patient and therapist variables in the treatment of low-income patients. *Psychological Bulletin, 8*(6), 344-354.

Maduro, R. (1983). Curanderismo and Latino views of disease and curing. *The Western Journal of Medicine, 139*(6), 868-874.

Maldonado-Sierra, E. D., & Trent, R. D. (1960). The sibling relationship in group psychotherapy with Puerto Rican schizophrenics. *American Journal of Psychiatry, 117*(3), 239-244.

Marcos, L. R. (1976). Bilinguals in psychotherapy: Language as an emotional barrier. *The American Journal of Psychotherapy, 30*(4), 552-560.

Marcos, L. R., Urcuyo, L., Kesselman, M., & Alpert, M. (1973). The language barrier in evaluating Spanish American patients. *Archives of General Psychiatry, 29*, 655-659.

Martinez, C. (1988). Mexican Americans. In L. Comas-Díaz & E. H. Griffith (Eds.), *Clinical guidelines in cross-cultural mental health* (pp.189-203). New York: John Wiley & Sons.

Olarte, S. W., & Lenz, R. (1984). Learning to do psychoanalytic therapy with inner city population. *Journal of the American Academy of Psychoanalysis, 12*(1), 89-99.

Padilla, A. M. (Ed.). (1980). *Acculturation: Theory, models and some new findings.* Boulder, CO: Westview Press.

Padilla, A. M. (1981). Pluralistic counseling and psychotherapy for Hispanic Americans. In A. J. Marsella & P. B. Pedersen (Eds)., *Cross-cultural counseling and psychotherapy* (pp. 195-227). New York: Pergamon Press.

Padilla, A. M., & Ruiz, R. (1973). *Latino mental health: A review of literature.* Rockville, MD: National Institute of Mental Health.

Ramos-McKay, J., Comas-Díaz, L., & Rivera, L. (1988). Puerto Ricans. In L. Comas-Díaz & E. H. Griffith (Eds.), *Clinical guidelines in cross-cultural mental health* (pp. 204-232). New York: John Wiley & Sons.

Ross, C. E., Mirowsky, J., & Cockerham, W. C. (1983). Social class, Mexican culture, and fatalism: Their effects on psychological distress. *American Journal of Community Psychology, 11*, 383-399.

Rotter, J. B. (1966). Generalized expectancies for internal versus external control of reinforcement. *Psychological Monographs, 80* (1, Whole No. 609).

Rozensky, R. H., & Gomez, M. Y. (1983). Language switching in psychotherapy with bilinguals: Two problems, two models, and case examples. *Psychotherapy: Theory, Research and Practice, 2*(2), 152-160.

Sandoval, M. (1977). Santería: AfroCuban concepts of disease and its treatment in Miami. *Journal of Operational Psychiatry, 8*, 52-63.

Senour, M. N. (1977). Psychology of the Chicana. In J. L. Martinez (Ed.), *Chicano psychology* (pp. 329-342). New York: Academic Press.

Sluzki, C. E. (1982). The Latin lover revisited. In M. McGoldrick, J. K. Pearce, & J. Giordano (Eds.), *Ethnicity and family therapy* (pp. 492-498). New York: Pergamon Press.

Stevens, E. (1973). Machismo and marianismo. *Transaction-Society, 10*(6), 57-63.

Stumphauzer, J. S., & Davis, L. C. (1983). Training Mexican American mental health personnel in behavior therapy. *Journal of Behavior Therapy and Experimental Psychiatry, 14*(3), 215-217.

Vargas, G. (1984, Autumn). Recently arrived Central American immigrants: Mental health needs. *Research Bulletin* (pp. 1-3). Los Angeles: Spanish-Speaking Mental Health Research Center.

Chapter 4

Issues in Working with
Southeast Asian Refugees
Dennis J. Hunt

In the late 1970s and 1980s the United States experienced one of the largest influxes of refugees in its history. In addition to the nearly one million legal refugees from Southeast Asia and other war-torn countries, there are between three million and five million undocumented refugees in the United States, the majority of whom are Hispanic. Most federal refugee assistance programs have focused on employment services and basic medical needs. In most cities undocumented refugees have been denied access to even these limited services. Very few resources have been made available to refugees who are having difficulty dealing with the traumas and tragedies of their past and the stresses of their new lives in the United States.

This chapter describes some of the more salient stresses and adjustment problems experienced by refugees and provides suggestions for working with refugees in a counseling situation. While there are some culture-specific examples, the discussion focuses on issues common among most refugees. Much of the information provided in this chapter derives from the clinical experiences of the author and the counseling staff of Connections, a cross-cultural counseling and foster care agency based in Falls Church, VA. No attempt has been made to provide a comprehensive review of the literature on counseling with refugees.

Stresses of the Refugee Experience

The essential feature of post-traumatic stress disorder, as described in the *Diagnostic and Statistical Manual* of the American Psychiatric Association, is the development of "characteristic symptoms following a psychologically distressing event that is outside the range of usual human experience" (APA, 1987, p. 247). While not all refugees exhibit post-traumatic stress disorder, nearly all experience psychosocial stressors categorized as *extreme* or *catastrophic* (as defined in the DSM-III-R). The following is a brief description of some of the major stressors common to the refugee experience.

Pre-Escape

Imprisonment. A very high percentage of refugees, especially males, have been imprisoned at one time or another. Many were held for long periods of time in deplorable conditions and experienced abuse from prison guards. Many Vietnamese males spent years in "reeducation camps" because of their affiliation with the United States government. Others were imprisoned for trying to escape from their country or because of their political or religious affiliation.

Death of family members. It is rare to find a refugee who has not lost one or more family members due to war, disease, or poor medical care. The family members most likely to have died are infants and males over the age of 15.

Loss of home and repeated relocation. Many refugees have left behind homes and land which had belonged to their family for generations. In many cases their homes were bombed and burned or were taken over by government forces. Many Vietnamese families that were forced to flee to the South to establish new lives after the French left Vietnam in 1954 became refugees a second time scarcely a generation later with the fall of South Vietnam; many narrowly escaped to the United States.

Loss of livelihood. Because war and political chaos usually result in the breakdown of a country's economic structure, most refugees experience a dramatic deterioration in their economic status prior to fleeing from their homeland. Many lost their jobs or had their businesses appropriated by the government. Businessmen and professionals often had to rely on their wives and other family members to perform menial jobs in order to earn enough to survive. These economic changes often had a devastating effect on the refugees' family structure as well.

Undernutrition. The collapse of the economy during wartime and political chaos produces not only a lack of income but a scarcity of basic foods. Most refugees have experienced long periods of undernutrition which may have serious long-term health consequences. Many babies are born of mothers with inadequate intake of calcium, protein, and other essential nutrients. These same deficiencies leave refugees vulnerable to a variety of diseases and, when combined with inadequate dental care, almost always result in severe deterioration of the teeth.

Physical abuse. Many refugees have experienced torture and severe physical abuse. Brain damage and impaired cognitive, physical, and emotional functioning often result (Goldfeld, Mollica, Pesavento, & Faraone, 1988; Mollica, Wyshak, & Lavelle, 1987).

During Escape and Processing

Illness. Refugees are often in poor physical condition and emotionally stressed when they escape from their countries. When this is combined with poor sanitary conditions and lack of adequate food supplies, they become vulnerable to a variety of illnesses. Anemia, dysentery, and parasites are commonly found among refugees who have recently escaped from their countries.

Robbery. Many refugees convert into gold whatever worldly possessions they have left before their escape. Thieves and pirates frequently prey upon escaping refugees, stealing this last remnant of their former lives.

Physical assault and rape. Whether they escape by land or by sea, refugees are very vulnerable to attack by criminals who may beat, rape, or kill them. These attacks often leave lasting emotional scars in those who are attacked or who helplessly witness such an attack.

Long waits in refugee camps. Many refugees must wait for months or even years in primitive refugee camps without knowing what the future holds for them. The initial hope and excitement that refugees feel after a successful escape often turns to apathy as they realize that they have very little control over their destiny.

After Arrival in the United States

Disappointment. Most refugees entertain many unrealistic fantasies about what life will be like in the United States. They are often disappointed when faced with the demands of day-to-day life in American society. They find that housing and food is expensive, that their inability to speak much English limits them to menial jobs, and that some Americans treat them with contempt.

Low social and economic status. Refugees are often forced to live at a social and economic level that is much below the one they enjoyed in their own country. Many must accept low-status, minimum-wage jobs and live in low-cost housing located in high-crime areas.

Language barriers. Limited proficiency in English handicaps most refugees and causes frustration in doing even routine chores. This is especially a problem for older refugees who generally have more difficulty learning a new language.

Role loss/ambiguity/reversal. Refugees are often forced to assume unaccustomed roles in American society. Since children generally become proficient in English before their parents do, they often become the culture brokers for their parents. Parents become dependent on their children to negotiate with landlords, utility companies, and store clerks. Women are often the first ones in refugee families to get jobs—either because they are more open to performing menial tasks or the available jobs are seen as appropriate for females only. These role reversals are often a source of conflict within refugee families, most of whom are patriarchal and hierarchical by tradition. Fathers left home to baby-sit frequently lose their credibility as authority figures; the mothers develop an outside network of friends through their jobs; and the children demand to be heard in the home as they become acculturated to American ways.

Bad news from home. Refugees are often filled with guilt and a sense of helplessness when they receive letters from family members remaining in their homeland. These letters frequently contain complaints about the harsh conditions of life and the need for large sums of money for food and medicine. Refugees who are struggling to make ends meet in this country frequently feel pressured to take on additional jobs to provide assistance to family members back home. They often become depressed when they are unable to earn enough money to help out.

Transportation limitations. In many regions of the United States the cheapest housing and the best jobs are in areas where there is poor public transportation. This situation forces many refugees to spend long hours commuting to and from work or to face the additional burden of purchasing and maintaining a motor vehicle. This is a particular stress for the many refugees who never owned or drove a car in their own country.

Discrimination/racial insults. Tragically, many Americans are not sympathetic to the plight of refugees and resent their presence in this country. Most refugees experience discrimination in some form and are the victims of racial insults, often coming from members of other ethnic minorities who resent the perceived special treatment given to refugees. In areas where jobs are scarce, there is often much resentment and even physical violence against refugees who may be willing to accept a low hourly wage. In schools, hard-working, high-achieving refugee students are often picked on by non-refugee classmates who are not as successful.

Woman shortage. There is a disproportionately high number of males among refugees in the United States. For example, among adult Vietnamese refugees there are approximately two males for every female. This imbalance means that many male refugees cannot possibly find a wife of the same ethnic background, yet many find it difficult to be accepted by women outside their own ethnic group.

Family composition. Many refugees do not have the support of the traditional family system after they arrive in the United States. All too frequently, households fall into one of the following categories:

Single Males. One of the most psychologically vulnerable groups of refugees is that of single males who have left their families behind and find themselves isolated in the United States, even within the refugee community. The imbalance in the ratio of male to female refugees limits marriage prospects of those men who would normally be forming families at this point in their lives. According to Kinzie & Manson (1983), this group is also at high risk for depression.

Female-headed households. A very high number of refugee households are headed by a single parent, frequently the mother. Many of these women have been abandoned by their husbands, while others are widows or unmarried mothers of Amerasian children. Still others reluctantly left their husbands behind, sometimes in political prisons or reeducation camps. Frequently these women come from cultures where females are not given the responsibility and independence needed to run a household alone. In the United States they rarely have the grandmother or other parental figure they would have turned to for assistance in their home country.

Composite families. Because of the scarcity of housing and the high cost of living in many areas of heavy refugee resettlement, unrelated families and individuals are often forced to share the same dwelling. This produces numerous stresses not only because of the crowding which occurs, but because of the confusion in roles and lines of authority it creates.

Child-headed families. It is not uncommon to find households consisting of young refugees 19 or 20 years old who have been placed in a parenting role and are expected to supervise numerous younger siblings. These young people frequently lack the experience and maturity to provide adequate supervision to younger children and are often experiencing serious adjustment difficulties themselves. Without the guidance of competent parental figures, the younger children in these families often drop out of school and become involved in inappropriate and even illegal activities.

Intergenerational value conflict. Most refugee school children learn English quickly and soon become immersed in American life. They want to dress as their peers do and may want to participate in activities which are in conflict with traditional family values. As these youngsters become more acculturated, the gap between the generations grows wider. In many cases, getting high grades diminishes in importance, the authority of parents is seen as less absolute, and parental decisions become open to challenge and negotiation.

Overcrowded housing in high-crime areas. Refugees often have no choice but to live in low-cost housing in undesirable neighborhoods. Many refugee parents try to keep their children at home most of the time out of fear that they will be harmed or become involved with other youngsters who will have a negative influence on them.

Legal status. Refugees who are in this country without proper documentation face the constant threat of being discovered by the police and being sent back to their homeland to face possible persecution and death. Undocumented aliens are also frequently exploited by their employers and are often blackmailed by individuals who threaten to turn them in.

Mental Health Problems Among Refugees

It is clear from the foregoing review of stressors commonly experienced by refugees that they constitute a highly vulnerable population in terms of their being at risk for mental health problems. Table 1 lists some of the most frequent mental health problems noted among Southeast Asian refugee clients seen at Connections. Most of these problems have also been identified elsewhere in surveys of refugee mental health problems (Coleman & Miller, 1979; Erickson & Hoang, 1980; Kinzie, 1985; Li & Coates, 1980; Starr, 1979; Sutherland, Avent, Franz, Manzon, & Stark, 1983; Vignes & Hall, 1979). While some of these problems are associated with the functioning of the family, others focus on the individual. Frequently the cases referred for counseling involve a complex interaction of several of these problems, as is illustrated in the case example which follows.

Table 1

Most Frequent Mental Health Problems
Among Refugees Referred for Counseling

Family Functioning
Marital problems
Parenting problems
Acting-out (teens)
Sexual abuse
Physical abuse

Individual Functioning
Cultural agoraphobia*
Identity confusion
Suicidal gestures
Depression
Somatic complaints
Post-traumatic stress disorder
Anxiety disorders

*Cultural agoraphobia refers to the intense fear and anxiety that some refugees feel when they are required to participate in day-to-day activities in American society. Inadequate English skills and a limited knowledge of American customs contribute to this phobia which can sometimes be so severe that individuals may refuse to leave the safety of their own home.

The Case of the Nguyen Family

Lien and Trang Nguyen (names are fictitious) were married four years before the Communist takeover of South Vietnam in 1975. Trang was 17 and a high school graduate; Lien was 29 and an officer in the South Vietnamese Navy. Before 1975 the couple enjoyed a good standard of living and the support of a large extended family. They had two children and seemed to have a happy future awaiting them.

The Communist victory changed life dramatically for Trang and Lien. Trang lost a third child due to birth complications. Lien was sent to a reeducation camp where he remained until 1980. Trang turned to family for support at first, but was soon forced to sell goods in the street market in Saigon to make enough to feed her children. She narrowly escaped being sent to work in the fields in the new economic zones, the fate of many of her friends and relatives.

When Lien returned home after five years in the reeducation camp, he was shocked at his family's living conditions and angered that his nine-year-old son and eight-year-old daughter were being indoctrinated with Communist teachings in school. He soon began planning for his family to escape from Vietnam. He gathered money for the trip from every source possible, including a loan from his elderly parents whom he promised to repay as soon as he got resettled in another country. Trang had become pregnant soon after Lien returned from the reeducation camp, so they decided they would wait until the baby was born to attempt an escape. During the TET festival of 1981, a son, Thuy, was born.

Soon thereafter the Nguyen family boarded an old fishing boat with 20 others who were determined to begin new lives elsewhere. The boat drifted for days on the sea. The food and water supply ran out, and the passengers became weak and began to lose hope. On the sixth day the baby died of dehydration. At dawn on the eighth day, their hopes rose as a Thai fishing boat approached. Instead, their worst fears were realized as Thai pirates boarded the refugee vessel and robbed and beat the passengers. Trang and the other young women were raped as the others stood by helplessly. Later that day a Dutch ship towed their boat into a port in Thailand where they were placed in a refugee camp. Eighteen months later Lien and Trang and their two children arrived in the States where they would try to begin a new life.

In July 1985 the family was referred to Connections for counseling. The local department of social services had been called in to investigate charges of physical abuse and child neglect. Hung, now 14, had been arrested for shoplifting and had been picked up several times for truancy. Police had been called to the Nguyen's apartment on several occasions to break up fights and Lien had been threatened with arrest for beating his wife. During the first counseling session Lien denied that there were any problems. He felt that much had been made of a small family dispute and that the only help they needed was with Hung who had become impossible to deal with and was the main source of family conflict.

Lien, who had not been employed since arriving in the United States, rarely left their apartment but had not assumed responsibility for household chores either. He had attended English classes briefly, but quit because he was not learning the language quickly enough. He had refused a job with an office cleaning company, citing numerous physical complaints including headaches and back pain as reasons for not working, yet he refused to see a doctor. Trang described Lien as having a nervous condition which sometimes led to explosive outbursts, especially after he had been drinking with his friends. She also reported that her husband often said that the family would be better off without him. She worried that he would leave them or harm himself. Trang's work as a maid in a hotel was the sole source of income for the family. Lien resented his wife working and became very suspicious if Trang was not home on time. Trang and Lien had not been sexually intimate since before their escape from Vietnam.

Lien was frustrated that life in the United States had not lived up to his expectations and blamed the United States government for the tragic outcome in Vietnam. He felt that there was no role for him in American society and felt that his son no longer showed appropriate obedience and respect because he had been corrupted by American values. He admitted that he lost his temper occasionally with Hung but argued that physical punishment was the only thing his son understood. For his part, Hung showed disdain for his father and spent as much time away from him as possible. He would sometimes not return home until evening, and frequently lied to his father about what he did with his friends.

Lien also admitted that he sometimes would strike his wife when she did not show the respect a husband deserves, but argued that it was a man's right to do these things in his own home. Trang was ashamed that the police and social services had become involved in family matters, but was grateful that someone had become aware of the pain the family was suffering and that help was being offered. Trang reported that she sometimes felt stressed to the breaking point and that she had no family or friends to whom she could turn for support.

Mai (the daughter) had taken on responsibilities far beyond those expected of most 13-year-olds. With Trang working longer and longer shifts at the hotel, Mai had assumed responsibility for the cooking, laundry, and even much of the food shopping. Mai and Lien enjoyed a close relationship although they often had fights about her dressing as American girls. Mai pampered her father whom she saw as needing her help and attention.

Lien was clearly a key figure in the conflict and disorganization which the Nguyen family was experiencing. He appeared to be overwhelmed by his sense of helplessness and angry at his life situation. He assumed little responsibility for what had happened to his family in the United States but may have assumed too much responsibility for the tragedy that befell them during their escape. He was depressed and voiced numerous somatic complaints which probably had no physiological basis. At 43 years of age Lien felt like a man without an identity. He had no role as a provider for his family, he had no position in the community, and was not even an effective parent. Lien was resisting the pressure to learn English, take a job, and move on with the next phase of his life. He was angry at the American social service system for intruding into what he, as a Vietnamese, viewed as family matters.

Hung received only negative attention from his father who served as a poor role model. Hung, angry at his father and at himself, had turned to his peers for support. He had already become involved with minor law breaking and was likely to become more of a problem for the family if they did not receive help.

Mai had assumed numerous adult responsibilities to help keep the household functioning. However, as a 13-year-old refugee, she had her own developmental and emotional needs which could not be long ignored without negative consequences.

Trang had learned to function effectively as a breadwinner, but had put other roles and responsibilities aside. She avoided conflict by working long hours and passively accepting abuse from her husband. As is so often the case with victims of trauma, she may have felt guilty and responsible for the loss of her two babies, the rape by pirates, and her inability to make life happier for her husband who seemed to be angry at everything, including her.

It is clear from even this abbreviated case history that each of the Nguyens was responding to the tragedies and stresses of resettlement in their own unique way within the context of the family. A few of the most salient clinical issues were highlighted here to illustrate the complex interaction of problems typically found among refugee clients, but this case example does not emphasize many of the cultural considerations which make counseling with refugees a challenge. Also not mentioned were the strengths, including the spirit of survival, which held this family together through the traumas they experienced. It is upon these positive qualities that the counselor must build in helping troubled refugee families become functional again.

Practical Considerations in Counseling Refugees

The diversity of cultures and adjustment problems represented among the various refugee groups makes it difficult to develop counseling guidelines which will be effective with all refugee clients. However, this section presents some of the practical considerations which have proven important in counseling refugee clients at Connections. The author recognizes that the refugee population is not monolithic. Refugees differ in terms of religion, education, class, political orientation, urban and rural lifestyles, etc. The concepts presented in this paper are offered as general guidelines to illustrate an enormously complex issue.

Structuring the Counseling Experience

The following guidelines can help the counselor structure the counseling experience in a manner that has proven successful with other refugee clients:

o   Provide a clear explanation of the counselor's role and what the refugee client should expect to get from counseling. Outline specific goals and ways in which the client will be helped. Many refugees come from cultures where the notion of mental health differs significantly from that held by Americans; in many parts of the world, trained counselors and other mental health professionals either do not exist or they deal exclusively with the seriously mentally ill.

o   Be explicit about your expectations from the client. Punctuality, honesty, cooperation, and frankness should be among the points discussed. Many refugees feel uncomfortable in communicating their opinions and feelings directly and forthrightly. Giving the client permission to be open and direct may not be enough. Continued encouragement from the counselor may be necessary.

o   Clearly explain the concept of confidentiality. Refugees who are unfamiliar with the role of a counselor may be unclear about how the information they share will be used. Since many refugees see involvement in mental health counseling as shameful, they must be assured that no one in the community, particularly the ethnic community, will know that they are in counseling.

o   Be directive and facilitate compromise in family situations. Refugee clients typically expect the counselor to be an authority and to have the answers to their problems; they may feel cheated if the counselor fails to provide clear direction and concrete suggestions. In family counseling situations, it is important not to violate the natural hierarchy within the family by advocating too democratic an approach.

o   Use professional bilingual counselors or paraprofessional bilingual co-counselors whenever possible (Kinzie et al., 1980). Although speaking the same language does not automatically assure trust and/or rapport, it does help to eliminate the disadvantage of possible cultural miscommunication. Children should not be used as translators for their parents since this may upset the traditional hierarchical relationship which exists within most refugee families.

o   When appropriate, use natural healers from the ethnic community, but don't perpetuate harmful superstitions. Many refugees strongly believe in spiritual and herbal causes and cures for their psychological problems, although they may be reluctant to admit it. In working with a refugee client who holds such traditional beliefs, it may be helpful to integrate these beliefs into the treatment plan.

o   Present issues within an educational context (e.g., a group session on "the perception and consequences of alcoholism in American society"). While most refugees may be uncomfortable with the notion of mental health treatment, they are usually more receptive to anything educational.

o   Don't overlook the possibility that refugee clients' problems may reflect cognitive limitations. A refugee's inability to hold a job and manage day-to-day responsibilities is often blamed on language deficiencies and emotional problems when in reality the task may be beyond the individual's level of ability.

o   Be sure the client has had a thorough physical examination recently, including speech and hearing tests for children. Physical problems such as anemia, hypothyroidism, or hearing impairment frequently underlie or complicate refugees' adjustment difficulties.

o   Ask refugee clients to explain how the problem would be handled in their own country. This may give the counselor insight into the client's expectations, as well as suggesting alternative approaches that may be successful.

o   Use elements of an individual's culture in developing a treatment plan. A Cambodian Buddhist who is suffering from survivor guilt may be helped by the thought that his survival is the result of good merits he has accumulated from a previous life; he may see that he was spared and others were killed because he has a mission which he must accomplish with this life. For a refugee couple from a culture where the woman is expected to be dependent on the man, the counselor may be able to help the couple redefine that dependency relationship within the American context rather than expect them to assume completely equal roles within the family.

o   Link clients with informal support networks to enhance the effectiveness of the counseling intervention. Most refugees come from countries where the extended family serves as the social service and mental health system for the individual. It may be possible to recreate a surrogate extended family for clients by linking them with supportive volunteers, church groups, or youth groups (Reny, 1987).

Establishing the Relationship

The following guidelines can help a counselor establish rapport with refugee clients:

o   For some clients it is helpful in establishing a relationship to refer them to agencies that provide advocacy services and assistance with concrete needs such as housing and day care. Many refugees enter counseling burdened with basic needs for food and shelter which must be met before attention and energy can be given to psychological issues. Helping refugees with their concrete needs is also a way of establishing a trusting relationship which will facilitate the counseling process.

o   In the initial counseling sessions, help the client not to feel threatened by the counseling situation. A counselor might offer to write his or her name for the client, and help in the process of learning to pronounce each other's name. Clients entering counseling may feel more at ease if the counselor engages in small talk before focusing on the presenting problem. Suggesting that a refugee client bring along a friend to the counseling session or providing the counseling at the refugee's home may also be less intimidating.

o   Avoid making assessments based on cultural stereotypes which often blind a counselor to the real issues in a counseling situation. Each family and individual should be evaluated as a unique entity.

o   Be cautious with self-disclosure. It may be perceived by refugee clients as inappropriate unless the counselor and counselee are of the same ethnicity or have shared similar traumas.

o   Be cautious in interpreting refugee clients' responses. Smiles, nods, and yes responses, especially from Southeast Asian refugees, may reflect respect and a desire to please, rather than agreement.

Strategies for Dealing with Specific Issues

The following guidelines drawn from the author's experience may also prove useful in counseling refugee clients:

o   Provide one-to-one systematic desensitization experiences for refugee clients who are suffering from cultural agoraphobia (Davison, 1968; Sherman, 1972). Start with an experience which will produce very little anxiety, such as a visit to a market run by individuals of the same ethnicity as the refugee client. Progress gradually to successively more stressful situations until the individual is able to use public transportation to get to work alone and function effectively in a job.

o   Help clients differentiate adjustment issues that are developmental from those that are associated with the refugee experience. Refugees frequently blame their unhappiness on adjustment problems related to the new culture and fail to realize that their relationship would inevitably have changed over time and that their young children would have become teenagers striving for independence even if they had stayed in their own country.

o   Help refugee clients to cognitively restructure their perceptions of past events which may have become distorted in their memory. Many refugees hold a distorted sense of responsibility for the tragedies suffered by them or their loved ones. The traumas they experienced may have shattered the assumptions they held about the world. They may doubt their former belief in the meaningfulness, fairness, and justice in the world. They develop a sense of helplessness as they come to realize how vulnerable they are and how little they are able to control events. Their sense of safety and security is threatened as they are faced with the inevitable dangers and unpredictability that life holds. Counselors should patiently allow refugee clients to tell their traumatic stories over and over until they have adequately pieced together events and successfully communicated the reality of their experience to the therapist. Counselors must help refugee clients redefine past traumatic events and help them make sense of them. Finding purpose in traumatic events often helps make them more bearable.

Conclusion

This chapter began with a section aimed at sensitizing counselors to the range of stresses common to the refugee experience. Specific mental health problems common among refugees were listed and a case example was provided to illustrate the range and complexity of issues a counselor is likely to encounter. The final section enumerated practical suggestions for counselors who will be working with refugees.

Although the complexity of issues involved in counseling refugees has only been hinted at in this brief overview, it should be clear from the material presented that counseling with refugees is an enormous challenge. Counselors must be sensitive to the stresses of the refugee experiences as well as to cultural differences relevant to the particular counseling situation. They must help people who may have lost everything to restructure their identities within the realities of life in the United States. The counselor who is not bilingual must also struggle with the awkwardness and inefficiency of communicating through an interpreter or using very basic English. Counterbalancing these obstacles is the fact that refugees, as a group, are remarkably resilient. The vast majority adjust reasonably well and many thrive on the opportunities they find available to them in the United States. Those who made it to American shores are survivors and have enormous potential for growth and change.

References

American Psychiatric Association. (1987). *Diagnostic and statistical manual of mental disorders, III-R*. Washington, DC: Author.

Coleman, C. M., & Miller, B. (1979). *National mental health needs of Indochinese refugee populations*. Bureau of Research and Training, Office of Mental Health, Pennsylvania Department of Public Welfare.

Davison, G. (1968). Systematic desensitization as a counterconditioning process. *Journal of Abnormal Psychology, 73,* 91-99.

Erickson, R. V., & Hoang, G. N. (1980). Health problems among Indochinese refugees. *American Journal of Public Health, 70,* 1003-1005.

Goldfeld, A., Mollica, R., Pesavento, B., & Faraone, S. (1988). The physical and psychological sequelae of torture. *Journal of the American Medical Association, 259*(18), 2725-2729.

Kinzie, J. D. (1985). Overview of clinical issues in the treatment of Southeast Asian refugees. In: T. C. Owan (Ed.), *Southeast Asian mental health: Treatment, prevention, services, training and research* (pp. 113-139). Bethesda, MD: National Institute of Mental Health.

Kinzie, J. D., & Manson, S. (1983). Five years' experience with Indochinese refugee psychiatric patients. *Journal of Operational Psychiatry, 14*(2), 105-111.

Kinzie, J. D., Tran, K. A., Breckenridge, A., & Bloom, J. (1980). An Indochinese refugee psychiatric clinic: Culturally accepted treatment approaches. *American Journal of Psychiatry, 137,* 1429-1432.

Li, K. C., & Coates, D. B. (1980, October). *Vietnamese refugees in British Columbia: Their psychosocial adaptation*. Paper presented to the Canadian Psychiatric Association Annual Meeting, Toronto.

Mollica, R., Wyshak, G., & Lavelle, J. (1987). The psychosocial impact of war trauma and torture on Southeast Asian refugees. *American Journal of Psychiatry, 144*(12), 1567-1571.

Reny, E. F. (1987, May). *Informal support systems for immigrants and refugees: A matter of survival.* Paper presented at the 13th Congress of the Society for Intercultural Education, Training and Research (SIETAR), University of Quebec, Montreal.

Sherman, A. (1972). Real-life exposure as a primary therapeutic factor in the desensitization treatment of fear. *Journal of Abnormal Psychology, 79,* 19-28.

Starr, P. D. (1979). *Adaptation and stress among Vietnamese refugees: Preliminary findings from nine communities.* Paper presented at the Conference on Indochinese Refugees, George Mason University, Fairfax, VA.

Sutherland, J. E., Avent, F. R., Franz, W. B., Manzon, U. M., & Stark, N. M. (1983). Indochinese refugee health assessment and treatment. *Journal of Family Practice, 16,* 61-67.

Vignes, A. J., & Hall, R. C. W. (1979). Adjustment of a group of Vietnamese people to the United States. *American Journal of Psychiatry, 136,* 442-444.

Chapter 5

Psychological Effects of Political Repression in Argentina and El Salvador

Manuel Orlando García and Pedro F. Rodríguez

The socioeconomic structure in Latin America, as in most of the Third World, is characterized by small minorities who own most of the sources of production and huge majorities who own nothing and are stricken with poverty, misery, illiteracy, sickness, and early death. Political repression is not an uncommon tool used by governments of both the right and the left to maintain their power. Persecution, torture, and murder—including increasingly "technically developed" methods of physical and psychological torture—have been introduced in the past 30 years.

This article explores the similarities and differences between the repressive methods used by the past military dictatorship in Argentina and the military governments in El Salvador; it looks at the psychological consequences on the individual, family, and community, as well as the different therapeutic modalities used in the treatment of their victims.

The first section focuses on the children of the missing persons in Argentina and on the mothers and other relatives of those victims of political persecution. The second section addresses the psychological problems experienced by Salvadoran victims of political repression, particularly refugees living in the United States who not only must adjust to an unfamiliar and often hostile environment, but who also may continue to suffer from the effects of past traumas and ongoing stresses.

THE ARGENTINIAN EXPERIENCE

In March 1976, a military coup overthrew the elected government in Argentina which was headed by Mrs. Perón. From 1976 to 1982 the military dictatorship mounted a "dirty war" under the pretext of exterminating subversion, but in reality aimed at wiping out all political opposition. Between 10,000 and 30,000 unarmed political dissidents were snatched away off the streets, from their homes, or from their jobs, never to reappear. The military government, acting in civilian guise with the help of paramilitary thugs, was careful to leave behind no official documentation of detention or imprisonment, rendering futile any attempt by relatives or friends to learn the fate of the *desaparecidos*.

64

At the same time that kidnapping, torturing, and imprisonment in clandestine concentration camps were being carried out by the Argentinian government, a multimillion-dollar public relations campaign was being waged to improve the image of the new government internally and abroad. The mass media helped effect an elaborate machinery of social silencing. To talk about the *desaparecido* or even to inquire about a missing loved one could lead to grave consequences. People who "noticed" that others were missing were themselves variously accused as "subversives," scapegoated as unpatriotic persons who were trying to discredit the nation, or characterized as being mentally deranged. Thus, not only were such inquiries futile, but one put one's own life in jeopardy and possibly that of the victim as well.

Torn between the unspeakable loss of friends and loved ones on the one hand and the imposed silence on the other, the entire society was victimized. The mental health field itself became a special target of persecution. Government-sanctioned psychotherapy was provided to help the citizenry cope with the loss of family members and others without a verifiable death, without a funeral, and without a burial. Psychotherapists who supported their patients' wishes to speak out for justice or to search for a missing relative were called agents of subversion by the dictatorship and treated accordingly. Dozens of Argentine psychologists and psychiatrists themselves "disappeared," simply for carrying out their professional duties. American and international psychiatric associations have remained virtually silent about this horror despite their being fully aware of it (Amnesty International, 1981).

The Catholic Church, with the exception of four bishops (one of them murdered) and a few priests, joined the silence and appeared to condone the government's actions by continuing with official religious rites. A predominantly Catholic population thus paradoxically became an involuntary accomplice of torture and murder.

In 1987, five years after the demise of the military dictatorship, the democratic government of Argentina belatedly convicted ten men from the military of human rights violations. Although this was a significant accomplishment, continued prosecution of such criminals is being resisted with military mutinies. The Catholic Church continues to preach forgiveness and reconciliation. The Argentinian democracy, squeezed by an increasingly defiant military and a bulging foreign debt, lacks the strength to prosecute the identified perpetrators of the kidnappings and killings. Not a single paramilitary group has been disbanded, and the new government is rapidly passing laws to appease the military and avoid a blood bath. In addition, the continued silence of the international community is not helping to bring about justice. Impunity from punishment of those responsible for the atrocious crimes against their compatriots perpetuates the insecurity of the survivors and their inability to resolve the situation which results in the psychological disorder known as victimization *(Meeting the Mental Health Needs of Victims,* 1987).

The Children of the **Desaparecidos**

Children of the *desaparecidos* include some who were taken into captivity along with their parents and many who were left behind by their captors. In either case, these children have undergone major psychological trauma.

Captive Children

Hundreds of children were kidnapped along with their parents, while others were born in captivity. (Many women were pregnant at the moment of their abduction, and others are thought to have become pregnant while in the hands of their captors.) As of May 1987, 41 of these missing children had been "found" and returned to their legitimate families, usually surviving grandparents (Abuelas de Plaza de Mayo, 1987). The credit for this work lies with the Argentinian human rights group known as the Grandmothers of Plaza de Mayo, who used a combination of self-taught detective techniques, available legal resources, and a newly devised method of "great-paternity testing" involving typing of blood.

A team of psychologists and physicians attends to the needs of these recovered children who, in effect, have been brought up by their own parents' captors (as masterfully depicted in the 1986 award-winning movie "The Official Story"). Preliminary findings reveal a surprisingly smooth and fast adaptation of these children to their real grandparents who, on occasion, allow for ongoing contact with the "captor substitute-parents." This uniquely tragic phenomenon is a source of important ongoing research that will surely provide insights into our understanding of child development and psychological trauma in years to come.

Abandoned Children

Far more children, perhaps as many as 10,000, were left behind by the captors when their parents disappeared *(Nunca Más,* 1986). Most are being reared by other relatives.

Dr. Norberto Liwski, a pediatrician and himself a victim of illegal detention and torture in Argentina, studied 62 of those children, ages four to sixteen (Liwski & Guarino, 1983). Two thirds of the children showed poor motor coordination while 60 percent evidenced hyperactivity and inability to concentrate. Other findings included a high proportion of intellectual and emotional passivity (71 percent), often leading to serious learning handicaps and disciplinary problems in school, as well as social immaturity (58 percent). The following symptoms were also common: constipation, psychodynamically interpreted as a fear to part with anything (43 percent); primary malnutrition resulting from not wanting to eat (33 percent); and higher-than-normal incidence of bronchial and ear infections (20 percent). Nocturnal fears, recurrent nightmares, and phobias relating to being alone or sleeping alone were also found in the majority of these children. A number of volunteer treatment centers have cited numerous cases confirming the findings of Liwski and Guarino. The disorders appear to be the result of a combination of four traumatic childhood experiences which make up what these researchers call the forced abandonment syndrome. This syndrome is caused by the following traumas:

Abandonment by one or both parents. Classic studies have shown that abandoned children (whatever the circumstances) tend to be subject to physical infection, retarded emotional growth, and blunted affect, especially when the loss occurs during the first year of a child's life.

Alienation from the surrounding community. Many of the families of the *desaparecidos* were ostracized by friends and neighbors out of fear. Teachers and others often told children that their missing parents had been terrorists. Because of the official silence imposed by the government, the word *desaparecido* itself became a taboo, often even amongst a victim's own family members. In an attempt to protect the children, many families worsened the alienation by offering implausible explanations such as, "Your father is away on a trip." Children felt the tension in their homes, yet any discussion of what had happened was avoided. Thus robbed of a sense of self, abandoned children often turn to a life of fantasy loaded with paranoia and demand impossible demonstration of affection.

Prolonged stress. The abandoned children's terrible uncertainty concerning their parents' fate and the imposed silence added to the stress of an already stressful situation. Stress was highest in those (of which there were many) children who had witnessed the seizure of their missing parents. They and the other remaining family members often lived in terror that the assailants might return. Such constant fear and trauma fixation can seriously retard a child's social, mental, and neuromuscular development (Garmezy & Rutter, 1983; Van der Kolk, 1987).

Physical abuse. The psychological effects of physical abuse, to which many of these children were exposed during the kidnapping of their parents, led them to develop the symptoms associated with battered child syndrome, thereby aggravating the other traumas. In all children, but especially in those at the concrete operational level (ages seven to eleven), guilt and self-recrimination were prominent since they tended to feel responsible for not having prevented the kidnapping of their parents. Children's capacity to develop guilt about events totally outside their control, particularly during this stage of development, has been described by several authors (e.g., Ginsburg & Opper, 1969), especially in reference to the loss of a care giver. Some boys felt rage and vengeance, entertaining fantasies about joining the army to learn their father's fate and to kill the perpetrators. It has been elsewhere described how traumatized girls tend to identify with the victim and boys with the victimizer (i.e., by becoming violent themselves) (Carmen, Reiker, & Mills, 1984).

Crucial to the treatment of these forcibly abandoned children was the need to overcome the secrecy inside their own families concerning what had happened and to enable them to share their experiences with other children and families of *desaparecidos*, as well as with society at large. The return of constitutional democracy in 1982 greatly facilitated this task. Yet learning the fate of their parents—which could be essential to the mourning process—has often proved impossible. Moreover, if their parents are to be presumed dead, the murderers need to be identified. Yet no killers are likely to be identified and brought to justice in the foreseeable future because the repressive machinery in Argentina has not been uprooted and retains great silent power.

The Mothers of the Missing

Mothers, as used here, includes the parents, surviving spouse, and other relatives of the missing who were affected by and responded to the political repression. In this authoritarian, male-dominated society, the first effective opposition to the crimes of the Argentinian military junta came from housewives—mothers demanding the return of their children. The "Mothers of Plaza de Mayo," who still march every Thursday in front of the Presidential Palace, acquired worldwide recognition and have been depicted in several books and movies (Bousquet, 1983; Muñoz & Portillo, 1985).

Psychosocial Effects of Repression

Absolute control of the mass media allowed the dictatorial state to mandate its ideology through a combination of partial information, misinformation, and intimidation achieved with random terror on any opposition. The emergence of new patterns of thinking and new operational models was observed among the population, with passive subjection being proposed by the state as a warranty of survival. People were, in effect, "alienated," as formulated by Piera Aulagnier (1977, 1980), assuming imposed values and ideas as their own. Drs. Diana Kordon and Lucila Edelman (1986) use the term "psychological induction" in referring to the influence of the repressive state on the thinking and behavior of the population. In their book, they mention these inductions:

Induction to keep silent. This induction, the most important one, has already been discussed.

Induction to self-blame. The families of disappeared youth were stigmatized as failing to raise their children properly. "How do you educate your kids?" and "Do you know exactly what they are doing now?" were phrases repeatedly used in TV, newspaper, and billboard ads. These questions were clearly aimed at reinforcing the guilt which is an inherent part of any loss or separation.

Induction to presume the death of the missing people. Many legal issues arose as a result of the undefined civil status of the missing victims, including management of property, widowhood, and declaration of wills. The Argentinian government promulgated a law to "facilitate" the resolution of these conflicts whereby disappeared people could be declared legally dead upon the request of a direct relative of the victim. This law, in effect, invited families to legally "kill" their missing loved ones. The psychological consequences of this induction are easy to surmise.

Induction to equate dissidence with antisocial behavior and/or mental illness. Unable to hide the public demonstrations, official propaganda depicted the marching mothers as a bunch of madwomen meeting in the public square. Opposition to the government at any level was considered unbalanced behavior and/or persecutory ideation. Many therapists, victims themselves of the imposed fear, would interpret all opposition to the dictatorship as self-destructiveness, anger directed at primary love objects, negative dependency, or suicidal behavior. (Indiscriminate opposition was certainly suicidal.)

Induction to equate disappearance with proof of guilt. "They must have been involved in something," many said of the disappeared. Conversely, people who were spared were seen as the innocent. Indeed, those who remained quiet and docile did not jeopardize themselves. During the trials of the "ex-commandantes" carried out after the fall of the dictatorship, tortured victims who were serving as witnesses were often inadvertently addressed as "defendants," revealing the long-lasting effects of this induction even during the new democracy.

Induction to forget. "It is imperative to forget the past to reconcile the nation," is the official government position. "Remorsefulness and revenge are not Christian," moralizes the Church. Such thinking leads to the avoidance of trials and the obstruction of justice.

Induction to disperse responsibilities. In an attempt to cover up responsibility for its actions, the massive official propaganda of the dictatorship frequently alluded to "shared guilt" in relation to any difficulty the country was going through. A television ad showing an ordinary citizen with the word "responsible" stamped on his forehead, for instance, was the government's response to Argentina's decaying economy. The "shared guilt" induction attempted to indiscriminately level active dissidents, silent dissidents, collaborators, and murderers.

Widespread Responses to the Psychological Inductions

The families of the missing were not immune to the foregoing psychological inductions. Some common reactions were the following:

Repression. In many cases, the family itself implemented a norm of silence. This pathological self-censorship inevitably resulted in hostility, guilt, somatization, and rich clinical symptomatology.

Suppression. Many families, while outwardly accepting the norm of silence, in fact preserved a good emotional connectedness with the victim—for example, by keeping every article of clothing, book, or piece of furniture belonging to the missing member. Some families would change the bed linen weekly and maintain an extra chair at dinner just in case the victim should reappear. Outside the family, nevertheless, the issue was never discussed.

Dissociation. Some families demonstrated a combination of attitudes showing identification with the enemy and, at the same time, preservation of the bonds with the victim. Such people would profess, "My son was innocent, but everybody else who disappeared must have been involved in something."

Self-recrimination. Bowing to the psychological induction to blame themselves, parents of the missing child would issue statements such as, "We should have educated our son (or daughter) in a proper way."

Indiscriminate resistance. Open defiance of the terrorist state by some relatives and friends of missing persons, which may have been motivated in some cases by survival guilt, often resulted in unnecessary self-defeating behavior.

Discriminative resistance. The team of psychiatrists working with the Mothers of Plaza de Mayo gave the name "discriminative resistance" to what they considered the healthiest response to the psychological inductions, as shown by this group of women, a small minority of the indirect victims.

The World Health Organization includes in the concept of mental health not only the recognition of reality, but also a creative, transforming, active attitude in dealing with reality. Freud in 1924 called normal, or healthy, the behavior that does not deny reality but attempts to transform it.

The Mothers of Plaza de Mayo dealt with the schizophrenogenic reality of the disappeared victims (i.e., their simultaneous presence and absence) by absorbing the ambiguity and uncertainty of the situation while demanding the victims' freedom. Their intellectual understanding of the political situation served as an effective defense of these women's ego integrity. Bruno Bettelheim (1973), a survivor of a World War II concentration camp, first described this way of coping with a catastrophic reality, thereby avoiding a narcissistic retreat.

It has been described how an impoverished relationship to the community perpetuates the vulnerability of traumatized families (Van der Kolk, 1987). However, when the community at large is victimized, adaptation to the imposed norms cannot be considered a measure of a healthy relationship since such adaptation would perpetuate the communal disease (denial, suppression, dissociation, guilt, disintegration, and fear).

The initial numbness, denial, and constriction of personality function following traumatization in adults (Kristal, 1978) could be prolonged interminably if the surrounding community in essence reinforces such numbing and denial. The ability to fit the traumatic experience into existing mental structures (i.e., to make it meaningful) has been described by Kristal (1984) and others as fundamental to the processing of new stimuli. Thus, through discriminative resistance, the "crazy" Mothers of Plaza de Mayo confronted the situation in a powerful and healthy way.

The Mental Health Response

A team of psychiatrists and psychologists spontaneously approached the group of Mothers of Plaza de Mayo who were seeking their sons and offered their services as an orientation group rather than as therapists. Some of the members of this mental health team had suffered indirectly the effects of the repression, although most joined them out of compassion and democratic convictions and the belief that the entire society was being adversely affected by the phenomenon of torture and the disappeared.

The team viewed its role as one of offering technical guidance about the use of therapeutic material that emanated from the victims themselves. While the

team identified strongly with the Mothers' ideals of justice (and therefore were
not neutral observers), the therapists recognized the possibility that idealizing the
women could block the team's ability to carry out their goals of support.
Together with idealization, attitudes of omnipotent repair on the part of the
therapist, sentiments of alienation and/or exclusion, and the need to talk about
the disappeared victim as if they were dead were all considered counter-
transferentially negative (Bozzolo, 1983).

Although many relatives of the missing needed individual therapeutic
intervention to maintain their capacity to function in a group, group therapy was
by far the most reparative and productive approach because it allowed for the
following:

Solidarity. Group therapy provided a support network for the victims'
families. This relates to what George Mead (1972) calls "sympathy," or the
development in the help-provider of similar characteristics to those receiving
help through means of understanding, empathy, and conscious identification.
Sentiments of alienation and exclusion were in this way ameliorated.

Respect for the self. This was intimately linked to the relatives'
preservation of self-esteem. Activities aimed at the recovery of the *desaparecidos*
improved the activists' respect for the self, as they bridged the gap between the
ego and the ego ideal.

Enhancement of ego functions. The following sentiments were
commonly heard in the support groups: "My concern is not any longer for my
child alone, but for everybody's children," and "What we do should contribute to
preventing the repetition of these atrocities ever again." Sublimation, by a shift
from a singular and immediate situation to a more abstract and universal concern,
contributed to the healing process.

Group analysis of the situation. This encouraged effective activism
as opposed to self-defeating extremism or obedient passivity.

Dilution of anxieties. This was a direct consequence of the interchange
of experiences and feelings that take place in a group.

Removal of guilt. The group could properly identify the aggressors as
external to the victims and help the family survivors detach themselves from
self-recrimination. In this case, "externalization" was not an unconscious defense
mechanism to cover up intrapsychic conflict by blaming unrelated environmental
factors, but rather the recognition of actual extrapsychic conflict.

At present (March, 1989), the fate of the vast majority of the disappeared victims remains unresolved. Mourning in this condition is unending. Meanwhile, investigation and prosecution of the disappearances have come virtually to a halt. In sum, to use the words of Drs. Kordon and Edelman, "The Mothers of Plaza de Mayo have managed to maintain their psychic integrity, but their wounds have not been healed" (1986, p. 149).

THE SALVADORAN EXPERIENCE

During the decade of the seventies, new social and political phenomena occurred in El Salvador. For the first time, the opposition parties (Christian Democrat, Social Democrat, and Communist) formed an electoral alliance to run against the army-backed official party (PCN). In two consecutive presidential elections (1971 and 1976), they defeated the PCN; however, the ruling apparatus denied their victory and responded with the hardening of repression. Opposition candidates were captured, tortured, or sent to exile while popular discontent protesting the fraud (strikes, public meetings) was dispersed by the use of massive force. The generalized disappointment with the electoral process, coupled with the growing social awareness, forced even the traditional opposition parties to look for other political alternatives, including the armed struggle.

In October 1979, following the overthrow of the Somoza dynasty in neighboring Nicaragua, an American-sponsored, broadly based civilian and military government rose to power in El Salvador. However, after two months, most of the progressive elements resigned, complaining that representatives of the ruling class sabotaged reforms and supported repressive methods. A civil war followed in which the Salvadoran government was described for several years by Americas Watch and Amnesty International as the worst human rights abuser in the western hemisphere.

The present political repression has led to the death of almost 70,000 Central Americans in the last seven years. This represents approximately 1.5 percent of the total population. Since 1982, violent death has become the chief cause of mortality, over and above death by infectious diseases, which was the principal cause of death before this period (Garfield & Rodríguez, 1985). Conservative data, at least four years old, show that some 600,000 Salvadorans fled to the United States after 1979, the year the war began there. Another 250,000 moved into neighboring countries in Central America and Mexico, and 500,000 have been displaced to other areas of the country (Lawyer's Committee, 1984). This means that one out of four Salvadorans is either a refugee or internally displaced.

The Use of Torture

Traditionally used methods of torture—such as *la capucha* (the covering of the victim's head with a tight rubber hood, sometimes containing irritating substances) and *el submarino* (repetitive submersions of the victim in water almost to the point of drowning)—are combined with newer, technically advanced torture methods such as selective beating of parts of the body (e.g., the ears) to produce both intense pain and equilibrium problems, thereby increasing the victim's experience of confusion and loss of control.

Another method is to apply strong electrical discharges to mouth, ears, eyes, and genital and anal areas. Psychological torture techniques are also used, such as giving information, true or otherwise, about the victim's spouse and children to induce guilt or increased anxiety and a sense of helplessness and vulnerability.

Forcing the prisoner to witness the torture of relatives and political peers, as well as mock executions, are other frequently used psychological torture methods. Such techniques not only intensify the victim's physical pain and psychological suffering, but they can be dosed in order to obtain the "maximum benefit" from the prisoner before the victim's elimination or transfer to another prison. In this respect, the information coming from the Salvadoran and Guatemalan prisoners is identical to the reports that came from Argentina during its years of military dictatorship (Allodi, 1980; Rivabella, 1986; Rodríguez Molas, 1985; Second Health Delegation, 1983).

The Appearance of Mutilated Bodies and the "Death Squads"

Whereas in Argentina the disappearance of the political prisoner *(el desaparecido)* was the cornerstone of the repressive apparatus, in Guatemala and El Salvador the appearance of the mutilated body (*el aparecido*) with thumbs and hands tied to the back lying on a city street or in the outskirts of a town is the identifying landmark of governmental repression. The violent capture, torture, and murder of political dissidents is carried out by military or paramilitary death squads. The use of death squads serves several purposes: first, to eliminate political opponents, while enabling the perpetrators of these atrocities to dissociate themselves from these groups and their activities, claiming to have no control over them; and second, to increase the general level of terror, confusing the population and instilling the fear of being punished by these extremely cruel, powerful, yet seemingly uncontrollable forces.

It is only the tolerance and cooperation of the government and the army that can explain the capacity of these forces to move freely in a highly militarized and controlled environment and to carry out their crimes with impunity.

Mass Murders by the Elite Army Battalions

Another landmark of political repression in El Salvador is the mass murder of adults and children. The mutilated bodies of men are typically left with their dismembered genitals inside their mouths, while pregnant women are left with their wombs opened and bleeding. This tactic is used as a reminder of the destructive power and punitive capacity of the military apparatus. Furthermore, aerial bombing of nonmilitary targets, including civilian populations, has been widely used by the government in recent years.

Broadening of Political Repression

Laborers, union organizers, and intellectuals critical of the dictatorial governments have been the traditional targets of political repression. However, the repression is now being used in both targeted and generalized ways. Nearly every sector of Salvadoran society has been victimized by the repression, including people long considered to represent sacred and unquestionable values such as Monseñor Romero, Archbishop of San Salvador. Professionals, including a significant number of physicians, nurses, and other health workers who denounced the kidnappings and murders of patients in hospital wards and operating rooms, were murdered or disappeared. Numerous journalists, teachers, lawyers, architects, technicians, and any group or person who could be considered "a threat to the security of the state," came to the same end. The broadening of the political violence has been the government's response to the increasing demands for justice and freedom.

Psychological Landmarks of Political Repression

Psychological Effects— Post-Traumatic Stress Reactions

Besides those people directly exposed to torture, most of the displaced persons have also experienced, directly or indirectly, the political violence. Several studies of Salvadorans and other Central American immigrants in the United States have found that more than a third of them present symptoms of post-traumatic stress disorder (Arroyo & Eth, 1985; Cervantes, 1987). Rodríguez (1985) found that 90 percent of immigrant Salvadoran children present anxiety, nightmares, phobias, depressive mood, and somatic complaints, all of them residual symptoms of the same disorder, in some cases five years after having been exposed to the traumatic event.

Post-traumatic stress disorder is a psychological reaction (not necessarily pathological unless it appears in a chronic or delayed form) almost exclusive to those people exposed to overwhelming and catastrophic experiences such as natural or man-made disasters. These include the reactions of survivors of torture and people who have witnessed the murder of relatives, those who have suffered persecution or had death threats made against them and their families, and other forms of persecution such as unannounced searches of their houses and, especially in rural areas, destruction of their property (including homes, crops, and cultivated land).

Other psychological disorders frequently found among Salvadoran immigrants are depression, anxiety, sleeping difficulties, somatization disorders, substance abuse, aggressive and antisocial behavior, marital conflicts, family violence, parent/child difficulties, and children's academic and behavioral problems (Alvarez, 1987; Cervantes, 1987; Vargos, 1984).

Family Disruption

Most of the recent immigrants from Central America to the United States had to leave their native country with little or no preparation and planning. Very often only part of a family emigrates, leaving the children or one of the parents behind. When and if the family is eventually reunited, children find that their parents have changed. If the parents remain together, both are usually working and cannot give the children the attention and help that would smooth the transition from one culture to the other. The children may find that the new house and the neighborhood are not as comfortable and as friendly as they expected. They resent these realities; they resent the previous abandonment by their parents; they resent being separated from the relatives who took care of them in their native country and whom they have grown to love. All this becomes a source of conflict which is often expressed in aggressive and acting-out behavior on the part of children (Alvarez, 1987).

The Long, Hazardous, and Expensive Journey

The trip to the United States itself can be a source of stress and traumatic experiences, starting with the economic cost. Because most of these Central American refugees cannot enter the United States legally, they have to resort to the services of "coyotes" who will take them by alternative and risky routes. The amount charged ranges from $3,000 to $5,000 or more, which often must be borrowed. During the trip, which may last weeks or months, the travelers are frequently mistreated, robbed, and raped by their guides. The final part of the trip, the border crossing, is usually done on foot or in the trunks of cars or trucks. At this point, many refugees are captured by the officers of the U.S. Immigration and Naturalization Service and either imprisoned, released with a high bail (typically $2,000), or deported to the country from which they came. Hundreds of would-be immigrants have died while traveling under these conditions, or else upon being sent back to Central America. Nevertheless, it is not unusual to find immigrants who have been deported five or more times.

Adaptation Difficulties

Adaptation difficulties are shared by all immigrant groups trying to integrate into the host society and culture. New communication codes, language, evident and silent behaviors, values, rules, and expectations have to be learned and understood in order to function effectively in the new environment. The longer this learning process takes, the longer the period of integration into the new society. Although this process of integration and adaptation depends largely on an immigrant's cognitive apparatus, emotional conflicts and disorders tend to interfere with and delay it. For instance, the initial fear of the unknown environment combined with the loss of self-esteem resulting from the lowering of their occupational and social status can produce anxiety and depression that affect the immigrants' cognitive capacities, limiting their search for alternatives and resources. Very often, immigrants have to take menial, poorly paid jobs in places that are a threat to their physical health. Many Salvadorans in the United States live in overcrowded and dilapidated apartments or basements. They typically live a very isolated and deprived existence, and their only source of gratification may be news from their families and the satisfaction of sending most of their earned money to them. Drinking or other drug abuse may be the only outlets to which they feel they have recourse.

Cubans, Southeast Asians, and other recent immigrants from Communist countries have been aided by federally financed resettlement programs which have facilitated their adaptation and integration into American society. Because of their undocumented status, many Central American immigrants do not have access to federally funded medical, educational, or food programs. Furthermore, the U.S. government does not consider them to be political refugees, but rather illegal aliens who have come to the United States for economic gain. As a result, they can be captured, incarcerated, and deported.

Fear of Capture and Deportation

The fear of capture and deportation is a pervasive and continuous source of anxiety, heightened by the promulgation of the Immigration Reform and Control Act of 1986, which threatens to penalize the employer who hires illegal immigrants. This has increased the panic and other anxiety disorders among these immigrants, forcing them further into hiding. As a result, most of them fail to utilize health services and other city and state programs available to poor people.

Many use homemade medicines since to resort to private physicians further decreases the undocumented residents' already-limited finances.

Unresolved Grief and Mourning

Pollock (1986) has postulated that the immigrant goes through a grieving process when leaving the motherland, similar to the one experienced when a love object is lost by death or other reasons. Freud (1924) described mourning as a process through which the loss of a loved one is progressively accepted and during which features and characteristics of the lost person are incorporated into the personality of the grieving person. Gradually, the psychic energy detached from the lost object can be used for new attachments. When this process is delayed or interrupted, it can produce depression, melancholia, and even suicide. In the case of an immigrant, the psychic energy detached from those who have died, disappeared, or stayed behind has to be used in the process of adaptation to the new society. If this process does not take place, the adaptation will be delayed and be made more difficult and the person will be more prone to develop depression and other symptoms (such as survivor's guilt) related to the unresolved losses. For Salvadorans and other illegal aliens, their undocumented status and the always-present possibility of deportation make the grieving for the fatherland more difficult. It is not possible to mourn, to accept the loss of a person, a country, or a reality to which one may be forced to return tomorrow.

Therapeutic Treatment of the Survivors

The Need for a Multidisciplinary Approach

The psychological treatment of the many Latin American refugee immigrants who suffered torture and trauma prior to coming to this country requires a multiple-problem-oriented response and a multidisciplinary therapeutic approach. Both the psychological and physical problems resulting from their previous traumatic experiences with life-threatening circumstances and external political violence, as well as their current economic, job-related, legal/migratory, social, and cultural differences, must be considered. The anxiety produced by their current situation can also interfere with and jeopardize the adaptation and integration process. Sources of current anxiety must be addressed in concrete ways by referring the persons to legal agencies to help with their migratory status, as well as to job training and employment agencies. Since Salvadorans and other Central Americans tend to trust church-related groups and these have proven to be effective in providing these kinds of concrete services, a system of referrals can be coordinated with them.

Psychological Therapeutic Interventions

In order to facilitate appropriate psychological intervention, every Central American immigrant asking for or referred for psychological treatment must be assumed to be a political refugee—someone who may have been exposed to torture or may have witnessed or experienced the murder of a loved one. An immigrant may claim to have come to the United States for some other reason, such as to seek better opportunities, in order not to be identified as a victim of political violence or an enemy of the United States.

From the very beginning of treatment, the therapist should let the immigrant patient know that he/she understands the pain and difficulties of leaving a loved and familiar country, and should encourage the patient to talk about the particular experience that led him or her to do so. The patient needs to know that the therapist will listen to anything that the immigrant needs to describe whenever the patient is ready to do so. This should be conveyed in a nonpressuring, supportive manner in order to reassure the patient that it is safe to talk openly.

Reporting a traumatic event serves several purposes. It has a cathartic effect of releasing the pressure of having kept inside not only the memory of the traumatic event, but also the associated feelings. When the patient reports the events, it is done with great pain, eliciting the same emotions experienced during the traumatic event.

This is also the beginning of another therapeutic goal: helping the person move from the position of a helpless and passive victim to that of a more active position of control. In El Salvador, the Catholic Church's Human Rights Offices are the only institutions that, while documenting the "testimonies" of the abused person, also offer this therapeutic approach—the recording of the violent experience. In Chile, therapists working with the survivors of political repression ask the victims to record their report of the event. The report is then typed and given back to the person to correct and edit. At this point, and only this point, is it filed. In Chile, this process is carried out in a more systematic way than in El Salvador, but both approaches serve the same therapeutic purpose.

Since many Salvadoran patients present at least some of the symptoms of post-traumatic stress disorder, one of the therapist's first tasks is to explain to the suffering person that his or her symptoms should not be confused with psychosis ("craziness"), despite the intensity of the persecutory ideas and nightmares and the intrusive and repetitive recollections of the event the patient may be experiencing. The patient should be reassured that any normal person in their place would suffer from similar symptoms. When patients still present symptoms five years after having been exposed to the catastrophic event, this cannot be exclusively seen as reactive to the event. Nevertheless, although the symptoms may appear integrated into the personality and the psychopathology of the victim, they must be treated as long-lasting and chronic effects of the trauma. Frequently, when targeted in this way, the nightmares, recollections, feelings of detachment or estrangement, and other complaints go away and the general functional level of the patient improves. Other therapeutic issues to keep in mind are the patient's fears (both real and irrational), the anxiety concerning deportation, and the depression resulting from the unresolved emotional losses.

Although it is helpful for a patient to talk about a past trauma in a one-to-one setting with a therapist, sharing the story with others in family sessions or task-oriented therapy groups has been shown to be more effective in decreasing and controlling the symptoms (Halbrook, 1987). Since the family has proven to be an effective system for buffering some effects of trauma, the reconstitution of the biological family or creation of a foster family (integrated with known and familiar persons) must be one of the main therapeutic goals, especially when working with children. Family therapy is an effective way of mobilizing the internal resources of refugee families to provide structure and emotional support to children and parents, especially when dealing with difficulties relating to social and cultural adaptation. We have found (Rodríguez, 1985) that the family, although efficient in fostering the intellectual and academic development of children, does not protect them against depression and anxiety. This is because the parents, having to deal with their own fears and unresolved losses, often cannot recognize the conflict either in themselves or in their children. Thus, the family approach to therapy is often the most helpful in such situations.

Finally, the participation of refugee patients in social and community activities such as sports and social clubs, church-based associations, and cultural and self-help groups is highly desirable. This helps diminish both a refugee's isolation and pathological behavior. Improved socialization and healthier adaptation can be achieved by promoting contact and support among Latin American immigrants, but even more so by increasing the nonpersecutory interaction between the refugee patient and other Americans.

Conclusion

Political repression in Argentina and El Salvador has produced enormous human suffering, immeasurable physical and emotional pain, and severe damage not only to the individuals, families, and communities directly affected, but also to the national psychological and social profiles of both countries. The sorrow and despair of the victims have been heard and felt thousands of miles away, and will impact this generation as well as generations to come who will have to come to terms with this tragic era.

The political repression in these two countries is similar in their use of new and more effective methods of torture and in broadening the social and economic spectrum of the people whom they victimized. However, they are also dissimilar. Argentina's repressive machinery followed a more covert path which allowed the government to distance itself from many of the events taking place. By isolating the victim's family from the larger society, it sought to reduce the use of legal recourse available to the family. The more overt repression displayed by the Salvadoran government is aimed at creating general panic and terror and speeding the disintegration and displacement of whole communities.

The goal of the mental health professional in working with refugees from these and other countries is not only to help the victim to reintegrate into the family and the community, but also to denounce these repressive practices and to work to eliminate their use. Associations of mental health professionals should join forces with other associations and human rights organizations to denounce torture used as a part of national policy anywhere in the world. Finally, medical associations need to take a stand and severely penalize physicians who participate in torture.

References

Abuelas de Plaza de Mayo. (1987). [Press release dated 5/27/87].

Allodi, F. (1980). The psychiatric effects in children and families of victims of political persecution and torture. *Darvish Medical Bulletin, 27*, 229-232.

Alvarez, M. (1987). *Report on mental health issues and services needs.* Task Force on Central American Refugees, Commission on Hispanic Affairs.

Amnesty International USA. (1981, August). [Public letter addressed to the Committee on the International Abuse of Psychiatry, American Psychiatric Association, listing names of 72 cases].

Arroyo, W., & Eth, S. (1985). Children traumatized by Central American warfare. In S. Eth & R. S. Pynoas (Eds.), *Post-traumatic stress disorder in children.* Washington, DC: American Psychiatric Press.

Aulagnier, P. (1977). *La violencia de la interpretación.* Buenos Aires: Amorrorto.

Aulagnier, P. (1980). *Los destinos del placer.* Barcelona: Argot.

Bettelheim, B. (1973). *El corazón bien informado.* Fondo de Cultura Económica.

Bousquet, J. P. (1983). *Las Locas de la Plaza de Mayo.* Argentina.

Bozzolo, R. C. (1983). Algunos aspectos de la contratransferencia en la asistencia a familiares de desaparecidos. In D. R. Kordon & L. I. Edelman, *Efectos psicológicos de la represión política.* Buenos Aires: Sudamericana/Planeta SA.

Carmen, E. H., Reiker, P. P. & Mills, T. (1984). Victims of violence and psychiatric illness. *American Journal of Psychiatry, 141*, 378-379.

Cervantes, R. (1987). Post-traumatic and psychosocial stress: The Central America experience. *SSMHRC Research Bulletin,* (Spring), 5-6.

Freud, S. (1924). Loss of reality in the neurosis and in the psychosis. In *Collected Papers, 2*, 277-282.

Garfield, R. M., & Rodríguez, P. F. (1985). Health and health services in Central America. *Journal of the American Medical Association, 254*, 936-943.

Garmezy, N., & Rutter, M. (Eds.). (1983). *Stress coping and development in children.* New York: McGraw-Hill.

Ginsburg, H., & Opper, S. (1969). *Piaget's theory of intellectual development: An introduction.* Englewood Cliffs, NJ: Prentice-Hall.

Halbrook, P. (1987). Salvadoran refugees and petitions for asylum: Clinical concerns. In *Political Asylum: A Handbook for Legal and Mental Health Workers.* San Francisco, CA: CHRICA and FMCARP.

Kordin, D. R., & Edelman, L. I. (1986). *Efectos psicológicos de la represión política.* Buenos Aires: Sudamericana/Planeta SA.

Kristal, H. (1978). Trauma and affects. *Psychosocial Study of the Child, 33*, 81-116.

Kristal, H. (1984). *View of information processing.* Paper presented at the Symposium on Psychological Trauma in Children and Adults, Boston, MA.

Lawyers' Committee for International Human Rights, Americas Watch. (1984). *El Salvador's other victims: The war on the displaced.* New York: Author.

Liwski, N., and Guarino. (1983, March). *Efectos seculares en el niño sometido al abandono forzado, en los niveles jurídico social y clínico psicológico.* Paper presented at the Fourth National Symposium of Social Pediatrics held in Argentina.

Mead, G. (1972). *Espíritu, persona y sociedad.* Buenos Aires: Editorial Paídos.

Meeting the Mental Health Needs of Victims. (1987, April). Conference on Implementing the U.N. Declaration of Basic Principles of Justice for Victims of Crime and Abuse of Power held at the United Nations headquarters, New York. (A/RES/40/34).

Muñoz, S., & Portillo, L. (1985). *Las Madres: The Mothers of Plaza de Mayo.* [Movie-video]. Los Angeles: Direct Cinema, Ltd.

Nunca Más. (1986). [The report of the Argentinian National Commission on the Disappeared.] New York: Farrar Strauss Giroux.

Pollock, G. (1986). *The mourning-liberation process and migration: Voluntary and coerced.* Paper presented at the American Society of Hispanic Psychiatrists Third International Symposium, Mérida, Mexico.

Rivabella, O. (1986). *Requiem for a woman's soul.* New York: Random House.

Rodríguez, P. (1985). *The psychological impact of migration and war on 16 Salvadoran children.* Paper presented at the Annual Meeting of the American Psychiatric Association, Washington, DC.

Rodríguez Molas, R. (1985). *Historia de la tortura y el orden represivo en la Argentina.* Buenos Aires: Eudeba.

Second Health Delegation to El Salvador. (1983). *Human Rights and Health Rights in El Salvador.* (Available from the New York Committee for Health Rights in El Salvador, New York.)

Van der Kolk, B. A. (1987). *Psychological trauma.* Washington, DC: American Psychiatric Press.

Vargos, G. E. (1984). Recently arrived Central American immigrants: Mental health needs. *SSMHRC Research Bulletin,* (Autumn), 1-3.

Chapter 6

Cross-Cultural Counseling
with Vietnamese Refugees
Kim Oanh Cook and Elizabeth M. Timberlake

For a variety of reasons, Vietnamese refugees have a limited understanding of mental health services. First and foremost, the very notion of mental health is rooted in the Western philosophical idea that rational thought and active intervention may alleviate human suffering. By contrast, the Eastern philosophies of Buddhism and Taoism prevalent in Vietnam accept human suffering and resigned waiting as part of the natural order. In addition, the Eastern philosophies place paramount value on the common bonds, mutual obligations, and helping traditions of family and community rather than on the individualistic orientation to life more prevalent in the West today. In view of these basic philosophical differences, it is not surprising that the conceptual structure and vocabulary of Vietnamese culture and language do not contain notions of psychosocial dysfunction and mental illness similar to those found in the United States. Nor is it surprising that many Vienamese refugees prefer to be discreetly cared for by their own families and communities rather than by outside professionals.

By the same token, many mental health counselors have a limited understanding not only of the differences between the cultures and helping traditions of Vietnam and the United States but also of the meaning of these differences in relation to the trauma, flight, losses, and resettlement experiences of their refugee clients. These knowledge gaps, together with the patterns of acculturation and accommodation built into many service delivery efforts, create barriers to treatment, problems and tension for both the Vietnamese refugees in need of help and their front-line helpers. The intent of this paper, therefore, is to provide a conceptual framework for cross-cultural counseling with Vietnamese refugees by, first, delineating the relevant ideal-typical Vietnamese cultural background, the trauma of the refugee experience, and stages of coping with the resettlement process; and, second, describing the roles and tasks of mental health counselors in assessing and facilitating the coping and adaptation of Vietnamese refugees.

84

Cultural Background

The cohesive and extended relationship network of the ideal-typical traditional Vietnamese family was explicitly structured and prioritized in a patriarchal society with women accorded lower status. Parental ties were paramount. A son had obligations and duties to his parents that were distinct and assumed a higher value than obligations to his siblings, children, or wife. Next in priority, sibling relationships were considered permanent and were frequently acknowledged in cooperative adult activities. Parent-child relationships were replete with themes of helping out the family, assuming responsibility, working hard, and achieving. All members of the older generation were responsible for transmitting guidelines for social behavior, preparing younger generations for handling stressful life events, and serving as a source of support in coping with life crises (Coelho & Stein, 1980).

In other words, the ideal-typical Vietnamese self was traditionally defined less in terms of individual characteristics than of family roles and responsibilities. These mutual family tasks not only provided a framework for individual behavior but also promoted a sense of interdependence, belongingness, and support. When given the material resources, the ideal-typical family had the desire and the person power to provide unconditional help to its network of kin. Traditionally, the rich took care of the poor; the strong, the weak; the healthy, the sick. In this way the family became the primary caretaker of its members' physical, social, and emotional well-being. The helping person might be a grandmother, an uncle, a brother, or a child. Built through long intimate associations, this helping relationship was a very personal one tailored to the specific needs of the family member. Thus in a sense, each extended family in Vietnam had its health, mental health, and social welfare system. As in all cultural traditions, however, there was diversity in the ways in which cultural values were operationalized by families. There were also families outside of the mainstream and in need of services not provided by family and community.

Religious teachings further emphasized loyalty, filial piety, and submission of the individual to the common good. The Vietnamese have evolved a basic philosophy of life, the *Tam giao* (three teachings), integrating Buddhist ontology, Confucianist ethics, and Taoist epistemology. These teachings offer moral and practical guidance which link personal, family, social, and biological levels of existence (Khoa, 1980).

In addition to meeting the spiritual needs of their members, Vietnamese religious institutions (pagodas, temples, ancestral homes, sanctuaries) ideally provided those helping services which a family lacked or was unable to fill because of its particular network of close relationships. Religious organizations (primarily Buddhist, but later Catholic as well), with their emphasis on compassion, tolerance, and social justice, provided counseling, concrete services, and institutional care for the poor, the sick, and the underprivileged when the family was unable to cope.

Both family and religion taught the art of self-control to each individual from early childhood on by means of rote learning of rituals (manners, customs), diversion from daily life (lullabies, music, poetry, nature, and contemplation), and punishment of deviant behaviors. Except among very close relatives or friends, open expression of emotions was considered in bad taste. To avoid confrontation or disrespect, disagreement, frustration, or even anger are usually expressed in an indirect manner by inference, silence, or a reluctant smile (Khoa & Van Deusen, 1981). The values embedded in this controlled coping style included self-reliance, resignation, self-respect, and suppression of unwanted emotions in order to maintain dignity.

In Vietnam, the traditional sense of belonging and moral responsibility extended beyond family and religious institutions to include the village community (Hanh, 1979). Until the beginnings of urbanization and the disruption of rural life by war in the late 1950s, each ideal-typical village was considered an autonomous entity and ranged in size from a dozen to several hundred families. Each had its own governing structure and was largely self-sufficient through agricultural or specialized trades. In the village community, every individual was guaranteed personal and economic security through village support systems which supplemented the services of family and religious institutions (Hickey, 1964; Kelly, 1977). For example, each village contained a network of health care providers (fortune tellers, matchmakers, and marketplace vendors). Their helping technologies were, for the most part, founded on nonintrusive concepts integral to Eastern philosophies. The concept of balance was of paramount importance in effecting cures. Deficiencies or excesses of bodily fluids and airs were believed to cause disease. The body was restored to a condition of balance or health by rubbing the surface of the skin or by swallowing therapeutic herbal substances (Egawa & Tashima, 1982; Tung, 1980).

Each village also served as a source of folklore, myths, and songs which were passed along from one generation to the next and served as rich sources of knowledge, insight, and ancient coping skills. But most important, each village provided its members with a common language which made it easier to seek help or negotiate with the social environment. In the presence of this historical continuity and shared commonalities, all villagers felt in harmony with their surroundings. Furthermore, in spite of the traditions, each member knew how to manipulate village rules and regulations through kinship connections in order to meet individual cases of special need (Van Deusen et al., 1980). This ability to manipulate the system gave each villager and family unit a sense of control over daily life and also fostered their adaptive capability. Although the urban area of

Saigon stood in marked contrast to these small rural communities, it too maintained many of these village traditions within its urban neighborhoods.

Today these idealized cultural traditions have passed from reality into the collective common memory of Vietnamese living in the United States. For those entering this country in the first wave of Vietnamese refugees in the mid-1970s, the memory of homeland cultural traditions may closely approximate the ideal-typical reality described here. For later waves of refugees, the destruction and chaos of war and the "reeducation" programs of the Communist regime had markedly changed the reality of these homeland cultural traditions but not the wish for a return to the idealized way it used to be. Indeed, for these later refugees, the collective common memory and the wish to restore cultural tradition is often stronger in the face of the double loss of remembered cultural tradition—first through the impact of the war and its aftermath and then through their flight from Vietnam to a new country.

Vietnamese Refugee Experiences

Although the specific uprooting experiences of individual refugees may differ based on their age or sex, there is a common experiential core. From the structured and familiar, albeit war-ravaged social environment of Vietnam, refugees escaped by land, sea, and air into unknown life situations. Psychological, financial, and other anticipatory preparations for the massive losses and changes accompanying the flight were usually not possible. Such drastic uprooting affected every level of their existence as individuals, as members of families and communities, and as Vietnamese. They suffered not only political defeat and loss of country, but also the losses of self-image and identity which accompany the loss of family members, support groups, reference groups, social roles, and vocational roles. Specifically, Vietnamese refugees lost some aspects of (a) the personal self-image acquired through the nurturing system of family and immediate community and (b) the social self-image acquired through the sustaining system of society's political, economic, and educational systems.

In the refugee camps, they underwent further separations from loved ones and experienced lack of privacy, segregation from society, and dependence on camp workers for their common human needs of food, clothing, and shelter (Liu, Lamanna, & Murata, 1979; Mamdani, 1973; Tyhurst, 1971, 1981). They also lost their sense of competence and the ability to control their own lives. For many, the frustration over their powerlessness in relation to everyday events and problems in living and their sense of hopelessness about the future was overwhelming. Often, the response was apathy and depression.

Upon resettlement, refugees experienced additional stress: loss of the relative security and structure of the camp as related to the common human needs of food, clothing, and shelter; cultural differences; language and communication problems; inadequate housing and finances; and underemployment (Ahmed, Tims, & Kolker, 1980; Lin, Masuda, & Tazuma, 1984). As strangers in a new culture, they encountered not only cultural and social dislocation but also varying degrees of understanding, acceptance, and rejection. Nor did the early refugee waves find a readily available Vietnamese community and support system during resettlement in their new country.

Resettlement: Coping   and   Adaptation   Patterns

Stages of Adaptation

Although the coping and adaptation patterns of individual refugees differ, observers have identified stages and styles of coping with the uprooting and resettlement processes inherent in flight. Even though these stages form a developmental progression, the intensity and duration vary as does the propensity to regress to earlier stages in times of great stress.

Stage of physical arrival. Initially, Vietnamese refugees tend to approach their new country with a positive outlook and high expectations about their new lives. During their first few months in the United States, their energy is directed toward meeting basic needs and ventilating about their war and camp experiences. Often, they suppress the pain of their multiple losses by massive efforts to reestablish their material worlds or by immersion in the daily expressions of ethnic life and community activities. Few symptoms of dysfunction are normally apparent (Tyhurst, 1971; Van Deusen, 1982), in part because little energy is available for dealing effectively with their massive losses and because the frantic activity involved in learning English, finding housing, and finding employment masks the depression. At the same time that the new refugees are struggling to obtain the material necessities and language essential for survival in the United States, they are speculating about their future return to the Vietnamese homeland and thus denying the finality of their new life here (Baskauskas, 1981; Coleman, 1980) and the permanency of their losses.

Stage of psychosocial arrival. Approximately six to twelve months after resettlement, however, the refugees' awareness of their losses and indeed of the disruption of their total life pattern typically begins to surface (Alley, 1982; Erikson, 1977; Marris, 1980; Meszaros, 1961). During this period of psychosocial arrival, they often experience acute distress and grief as they face their losses and social displacement and idealize the past. Refugees (like other people in stressful situations) express their distress through a wide array of symptoms: feelings of guilt, feelings of inadequacy, hypersensitivity, tension, fatigue, temperamental behavior, fluidity of mood, general feelings of disequilibrium and disorientation, lack of sense of continuity of self, impaired interpersonal skills, marital and intergenerational conflict, and various somatic complaints (Brown, 1982; Lin, Carter, & Kleinman, 1985; Lin, Tazuma, & Masuda, 1979; Masuda, Lin, & Tazuma, 1980; Mattson & Ky, 1978). Depending upon the personality structure, interpersonal supports, environmental supports, and degree of life stress encountered, individual refugees may experience these symptoms as transitory or long lasting, as mild or severe.

Stage of reality confrontation. After about two years, refugees often begin to reformulate their grief and constructively channel it into helping those left behind. During this third stage, they idealize their former life in Vietnam less and less and begin to perceive the realities of life in the United States more clearly. They become increasingly aware that the old patterns of coping and adaptation which sustained them at home are no longer sufficient (Carza-Guerrero, 1974; Cohon, 1981; Marris, 1974, 1980; Mathers, 1974). They have usually begun to acquire a working knowledge of English, the ability to perform new roles, and the ability to handle new situations as they occur. Many have acquired employment or are enrolled in educational programs. As the refugees develop a new perception of themselves and their roles in their new country, they begin to develop a new identity (Finnan, 1981; Lin et al., 1979; Masuda et al., 1980; Silver & Chui, 1985). As they learn the cultural patterns of the United States, they shift from participation primarily in the institutions of their new ethnic community to participation in other institutions as well.

Stage of settling in. Less dramatic change in refugee adjustment occurs after the four- to five-year mark. Language skills and cultural knowledge have been acquired. Occupational skills have been utilized or redirected. The massive drive and strong determination to achieve have lessened somewhat, and hope is transferred to the achievements of the next generation (Boman & Edwards, 1984; Carza-Guerrero, 1974; Masuda et al., 1980; Mathers, 1974). (The issues of the next generation in relation to refugee adjustment are beyond the scope of this paper.)

Stage of socioeconomic stability. After about seven to ten years in the United States, stability in socioeconomic status is achieved and improvement continues gradually. In the process of achieving stability, some Vietnamese maintain positive beliefs about themselves, the world, and the future. For this group, assessing themselves and their abilities and taking appropriate risks to better their lives has become an adaptive way of life. In the process, they often band together with selected other Vietnamese to pool resources and invest in their collective future. Too, their energies are redirected from focusing on their own survival into strengthening their ethnic community within the multicultural context of the United States. For others, however, their sense of well-being deteriorates and their beliefs about self, the world, and the future become negativistic as they confront their lowered socioeconomic status and their current cultural and social environment. They begin to feel powerless in the face of day-to-day happenings. They perceive themselves as failures in the land with the mythology of opportunity. They feel alienated from past cultural traditions and isolated from the collective common memory of these traditions. Survival guilt once again comes to the forefront with a concomitant anger toward deceased family members and ambivalence about their current lives. In summary, this latter group is experiencing a depressive reaction. For some Vietnamese, this reaction is strong and acute; for others, milder.

Individual Coping Mechanisms

The preceding description of the stress-provoking conditions which refugees experience and the stages in their adaptation raises questions about how individual refugees cope with this stress and its impact on their mental health. For example: How do they cope with the immediate implications of stressful events? How do they try to make some meaning of these experiences of uprooting and resettlement in terms of integration into their ongoing lives? In the face of these continuing environmental demands on the personal resources of individual refugees, coping and adaptation take many forms, including (a) active problem-solving efforts directed at mastery of a stressful event, (b) efforts to manage the subjective feelings associated with the stress, (c) efforts to accommodate one's self to changed circumstances which prove intransigent to change or mastery, and (d) defensive efforts to deny the full impact of the stressful life events and life conditions. Many refugees use a variety of these forms and cope successfully with both major and minor stress. The primarily defensive coping efforts of others, however, are dysfunctional (Choken-Owan, 1985).

Frequent dysfunctional coping patterns include the use of two physiological systems (respiratory and digestive) as primary somatic targets (Lin et al., 1979; Masuda et al., 1980). These and other illnesses frequently cluster around the two-year mark after refugee flight occurred (Holmes & Masuda, 1973; Lin et al., 1985). Moreover, refugees who initially respond to the flight and resettlement with many physical symptoms tend to maintain that pattern (Lin et al., 1985; Rahe, Looney, Ward, Tung, & Liu, 1978; Silver & Chui, 1985).

Denial, the defense mechanism most frequently used by Vietnamese refugees (Smither & Rodríguez-Giegling, 1979), is originally adopted to help lessen the impact of the uprooting and to allow refugees to get on with the task of survival. However, continued use of this defense mechanism is likely based on its congruence with the Vietnamese cultural values of self-sacrifice, submission, harmony, and fate. Nevertheless, when its use fails to shield a refugee from some of the harsh realities of the uprooting and resettlement processes and when massive support is not available, psychosocial dysfunction may occur (Kinzie & Manson, 1983). For example, an assessment of the mental health needs of Indochinese refugees (Pennsylvania Dept. of Public Welfare, 1979) spelled out some alarming findings: (a) many mental health problems among Vietnamese refugees who arrived in 1975 only began to surface five years later; (b) depression was the most frequently reported problem; and (c) anxiety, marital conflict, and intergenerational conflict were prevalent. At one extreme, the psychosocial dysfunction or mental health problems may take the form of uprooting psychosis (Lin et al., 1984; Pfister-Ammende, 1973). At the other extreme, suicide may be perceived as the ultimate solution to life's problems (Alley, 1982). Indeed, news media reports from the mid-1980s identify an increase in Vietnamese male suicides.

Family Coping Patterns

Family patterns of coping and adaptation are also apparent among Vietnamese refugees (Haines, Rutherford, & Thomas, 1981). Family units react to this life crisis of uprooting and separation by seeking to mend or reconstitute their traditional structures as rapidly as possible. For example, families split apart during evacuation and resettlement work hard at rebuilding a social network through incorporating distant relatives, friends, and even strangers who are also refugees. (Indeed the phenomenon of being in the same boat seems to generate strong mutual support among refugees.) As more members are incorporated into the family unit, the economic burden becomes a shared stress and the functions of the Vietnamese extended family are gradually restored.

As internal resources once again become available to the reconstituted unit, the family strives to maintain or reestablish Vietnamese traditions. The family resumes caring for the young, teaching traditional values, and investing in future generations. Many Vietnamese children are now excelling in high school and college. Family members extol self-sacrifice, suppression of emotions, and problem-solving without external intervention. Together, they share feelings of nostalgia for the old days and make efforts to keep in touch with family members who remain in Vietnam.

Along with these adaptive coping patterns, however, problematic behaviors have also become apparent in many Vietnamese refugee families. Anxious about their diminished authority, some grandparents and parents resort to autocratic rules, scapegoating of more vulnerable members (such as the elderly, the less functional, or a spouse), and resisting of outside influences. In other words, they have become defensively conservative, having been so suddenly faced with a strange culture which in many respects appears to be a menace to the survival of their own system of values (Khoa & Van Deusen, 1981). In the face of such family tensions some youngsters rebel and act out against the traditional family values and cultural expectations. In other families, marked dependency needs of individual members become apparent in an "I'm taking care of the world" lifestyle. Many of these families continue to rely on available community supports and struggle to meet their own subsistence needs, while individual family members simultaneously send large amounts of money back to the Vietnamese homeland. In their efforts to take care of the world "that used to be," these individuals are in a sense not only meeting their own dependency needs but also allaying their guilt about surviving.

Community Building

In addition to seeking to reconstitute the traditional family structure, refugees also seek to locate and build Vietnamese communities in their new country. Although the existing U.S. sponsorship system has scattered the 461,000 Vietnamese refugees (who arrived since 1975) throughout the country, most refugees have managed to get in touch with as many family members and acquaintances as possible (*Refugee Reports,* 1985). They gather together in small groups to exchange information, commiserate over their present circumstances, and mourn their losses. This search for a support system and traditional community network has gradually given rise to a pattern of secondary migration (Bach, 1979; Montero, 1979; *Refugee Reports,* 1985). Growing Vietnamese communities in Texas, Louisiana, California, and the greater metropolitan area of the District of Columbia provide evidence of this migration.

In its turn, the new community pulls together all of the available Vietnamese resources in order to form an identifiable ethnic support system. Religious groups, friendship groups, extended families, mutual assistance associations, and groups of professionals band together. Traditional activities such as Vietnamese holidays, religious ceremonies, ethnic food and banquets, and mahjong clubs become ritualistic experiences which restore a sense of normalcy to disrupted lives. In a sense, these traditional rituals minimize the changes which have occurred and transform the individually experienced refugee and resettlement crises into a socially recognized predicament (Back, 1980). Although geographic distance, economic factors, and lack of clear leadership initially inhibited community growth, the new Vietnamese communities have slowly begun to serve as a forum for cathartic collective mourning of losses and a buffer between the old familiar lifestyle and the new modern one which is physically accessible but often emotionally unacceptable to the refugees.

According to Back (1980), the attachment of refugees to these new community groupings serves to maintain their old identity until a newer identity and clearer status within the United States is worked out. Although the outcomes of the acculturation of Vietnamese refugees are unknown, studies of other ethnic groups suggest the availability of many alternatives. Among them are assimilation, coexistence, or integration into a pluralistic society (Coelho & Ahmed, 1980; Kleinman, 1980; Zwingmann & Pfister-Ammende, 1973).

Model for Cross-Cultural Counseling

Assessment

The foregoing delineation of Vietnamese refugee experiences and stages of coping with the refugee process provide a framework for assessing (a) the strengths and weaknesses of individual refugees; (b) their coping and adaptation patterns, as well as stages of adaptation; and (c) their family and community support networks. Psychosocial assessment includes a detailed social history of the clients' war and refugee experiences, camp and transit experiences, and recent trauma experiences in relation to gender identity as well as age and developmental stage at the time of these stressful experiences. More traditional information includes: presenting problem, solutions attempted, family and personal history and losses, language skills, current socioeconomic status and employment situation, support network of family and friends, and general quality of life. Careful assessment identifies points of entry into the helping process and treatment strategies that individualize the refugee in need of assistance.

Concrete Services

The first line of service provision is assuring that the basic human needs for food, clothing, and shelter are met. In a Vietnamese helping context, provision of concrete assistance takes on an interpretation of care and sharing among kin. Thus, concrete service needs identified by a refugee family provide a functional role for the counselor which is easier for the refugee client to understand. In meeting concrete service needs, a directive, structured counseling style is often helpful. Such a style is congruent with the well-defined role obligations and expectations of traditional Vietnamese culture and family structure. By focusing on doing and thinking rather than on feeling, this style allows for the characteristic Vietnamese emotional restraint in confronting personal problems and does not move prematurely to the affective level.

Social Skills

Along with meeting basic human needs, a core component of service delivery is providing access to survival tools such as English, employment skills, and other social skills. Learning social skills involves both positive and negative aspects. On the positive side, refugees need to learn to take advantage of existing opportunities for education, job training, and social/economic mobility and to integrate compatible American values with their Vietnamese values. For example, competition in education and employment may be viewed as strengthening the individual and the family unit. On the negative side, refugees need to learn where Americans are vis-a-vis the Vietnam war experience as well as in relation to refugees. They also need to be aware of socialization forces and to maintain their own cultural identity within the context of this multicultural society.

Counseling

Mental health goals with this population-at-risk include helping Vietnamese refugee clients cope effectively with their present social situation. First, as persons caught in the middle between the old familiar Vietnamese culture and the strange new cultures of pluralistic America, refugees must make sense out of the contradictory habits and beliefs to which they are regularly exposed (Berry, 1980; Kleinman, 1980; Park, 1928; Stonequist, 1935). Second, as persons who have experienced the trauma inherent in being uprooted from their homeland and resettled in a different country, they must come to grips with their multiple losses. Unless these crucial tasks are satisfactorily accomplished, refugees are likely to evidence psychosocial dysfunction (Mokuau, 1987). Dysfunction associated with difficulty completing the first task is likely to include confusion in thought, affect, and behavior; with the second, somatic and affective symptoms of depression. Culturally relevant counseling in these instances begins with helping refugee clients look into their past to identify (a) supportive resource persons who were helpful in times of stress, their qualities as helpers, and their helping techniques; (b) family and community structures which were helpful in times of stress; (c) the refugee's own adaptive coping pattern in the face of change; and (d) the refugee's learning style.

In addition to using this information as part of the psychosocial assessment, the mental health counselor can use it to engage the refugee in problem-solving, rebuilding a support network, and constructing creative and culturally relevant intervention techniques. For instance, Vietnamese teaching-learning situations often include setting examples and following examples set by teachers and peers. Therefore, mental health intervention techniques of role modeling and role playing provide familiar ways of learning to cope with the role changes associated with acculturation and with the present social situation. Portrayal of social functioning in past and present cultures through these techniques involves a dynamic interactive process between the refugee and the counselor as each (a) brings knowledge to bear on the problem at hand, (b) anticipates future contingencies, and (c) rehearses alternative approaches to these contingencies. Their mutual objective in this process is to bring together past and present chaos in the service of the refugee's future functioning in the United States. Moreover, by portraying future situations, refugees may begin to think that there is a real future for themselves and their children here.

Restoring refugee clients' personal and social self-image and feelings of competence are additional mental health goals which complement the goal of effective coping. However, since the personal self-image of a Vietnamese individual is intricately woven into the family image, culturally relevant intervention strategies are family-centered. For example, the Vietnamese family-image, and therefore personal self-image, includes such traditional values as resilience, patience, and respect for authority as well as a sense of duty toward family and community. Restorative mental health intervention techniques, consequently, are aimed at (a) restoring an orderly network of hierarchical family relationships, (b) learning new roles and modifying traditional family functions, (c) restructuring the refugee family's perception of itself as an incomplete extended family unit into an altered but functional family system, and (d) building a sense of belonging to a new community. However, a mental health counselor can enter into a Vietnamese family system only after a role for the counselor has been established. For example, a counselor who offers concrete mental health services to meet needs identified by the family has a familiar functional role reflective of sharing among relatives.

The professional helping relationship must also be in keeping with the Vietnamese tradition of a personal helping relationship tailored to meet individual needs and must take into account resistance to participating in services. Thus, in the tradition of settlement house work, the effective mental health counselor must become intimately associated with refugee clients' families and communities. In the process, the counselor assumes the traditional family or community role of helper with its concomitant duties. This creates obligations for investment of self and time that often go beyond the usual demands of the profession. Once engaged in a refugee's support network, the mental health counselor becomes part of a rigid role system which expects that role relationships remain the same through time and space both in periods of crisis and peacefulness. Time-limited and work-oriented professional behavior (for example, ending a counseling session just because the allotted time is up) is not understood by Vietnamese refugees. Neutrality and objectivity on the part of a counselor tend to be translated as disinterest, coldness, disrespect, and even betrayal. Moreover, given their emphasis on harmony, many Vietnamese clients have difficulty discussing their problems and sharing their feelings and concerns. If a counselor attempts to focus on a client's personal inner world too early in the counseling relationship, the client may abruptly and prematurely withdraw from counseling. By the same token, too abrupt an exit by the mental health counselor from a refugee's support network may be interpreted as betrayal of trust or disloyalty. Thus, unless the process of terminating counseling is carefully worked through, this newest loss may undo the goals achieved.

A counselor can help Vietnamese refugee clients restore their social self-image by helping them connect with existing community support systems and build needed new ones. For example, mental health counselors may need to connect refugees with institutions which can help meet their spiritual needs—such as churches, pagodas, and temples. Connecting refugee children and their families with educational institutions is likely to involve mediation, advocacy, and sharing information about both cultures to all concerned. Counselors may also encourage the emergence of natural leaders within the Vietnamese community and support the development of significant social structures such as family associations and cultural activity groups. In addition, counselors need to assess the overall social situation resulting from the addition of refugees to a particular community and the diversity among the refugees, as well as work on tensions between new and old residents in relation to issues such as employment, housing, and resource allocation.

Community Mobilization

The Vietnamese communities that have emerged as part of the secondary migration and as part of the support systems of refugee families today represent untapped potential. They provide a means for maintaining the Vietnamese refugees' cultural heritage as well as a means for building bridges with the multicultural American heritage. One bridge, for example, would involve setting Vietnamese refugee experiences in the context of the experiences of other immigrant groups in the United States. Another bridge would help Vietnamese communities build connections with mainstream business and political organizations in the larger community. A third bridge might involve connecting the Vietnamese community mental health care traditions with the more recently developed American community mental health services in order to develop culturally sensitive services.

Conclusion

Taft, North, and Ford (1979) view resettlement of refugees as the process of finding a new home, obtaining adequate employment, and developing the ability to function in a new society, while retaining a sense of appreciation and pride for one's cultural heritage. From this perspective, refugees should be viewed as persons who are momentarily out of step with the dominant culture in their new homeland and not as persons who will be permanently dependent. Thus, most refugees are temporarily unemployed or underemployed and in need of specialized types of support systems (such as housing, language training, cultural orientation, and help in transferring or developing occupational skills and career identity). To facilitate their efforts to cope and adapt and to provide them with the tools for achieving the long-range goal of self-sufficiency, refugees need culturally sensitive and culturally relevant health, mental health, educational, and social services.

Note: Reprinted by permission of NASW. An earlier version of this chapter was published in Social Work, *March-April 1984, 29(2), 108-113.*

References

Ahmed, P., Tims, F., & Kolker, A. (1980). After the fall: Indochinese refugees in the United States. In G. Coelho & P. Ahmed (Eds.), *Uprooting and development* (pp. 497-512). New York: Plenum Press.

Alley, J. (1982). Life threatening indicators among Indochinese refugees. *Suicide and Life Threatening Behavior, 12,* 46-51.

Bach, R. (1979). *Secondary migration of Indochinese refugees to Los Angeles, California.* Washington, DC: Brookings Institution.

Back, K. (1980). Uprooting and self-image: Catastrophe and continuity. In G. Coelho & P. Ahmed (Eds.), *Uprooting and development* (pp. 117-130). New York: Plenum Press.

Baskaukas, L. (1981). The Lithuanian refugee experience and grief. *International Migration Review, 15*(1-2), 276-291.

Berry, J. (1980). Acculturation as varieties of adaptation. In A. Padilla (Ed.), *Acculturation theory, models, and some new findings.* Boulder: Westview Press.

Boman, B., & Edwards, M. (1984). The Indochinese refugee: An overview. *Australian and New Zealand Journal of Psychiatry, 18,* 40-52.

Brown, G. (1982). Issues in the resettlement of Indochinese refugees. *Social Casework, 63*(3), 155-159.

Carza-Guerrero, C. (1974). Culture shock: Its mourning and the vicissitudes of identity. *American Psychoanalytic Association Journal, 22,* 408-429.

Choken-Owan, T. (1985). *Southeast Asian mental health: Treatment, prevention, services, training and research.* Washington, DC: NIMH in cooperation with Office of Refugee Resettlement, U.S. Dept. of HHS.

Coelho, G., & Ahmed, P. (Eds.). (1980). *Uprooting and development.* New York: Plenum Press.

Coelho, G., & Stein, J. (1980). Change, vulnerability, and coping: Stresses of uprooting and overcrowding. In G. Coelho & P. Ahmed (Eds.), *Uprooting and development* (pp. 19-40). New York: Plenum Press.

Cohon, D. (1981). Psychological adaptation and dysfunction among refugees. *International Migration Review, 15*(1-2), 255-275.

Coleman, C. (1980). Mental health problems of Indochinese refugees in the United States. *Refugees and Human Rights Newsletter, 4,* 3.

Egawa, J., & Tashima, N. (1982). *Indochinese healers in Southeast Asian refugee communities.* San Francisco: Pacific Asian Mental Health Research Project.

Erikson, E. (1977). *Choice and reason: Stages in the ritualization of experience.* New York: Norton Press.

Finnan, C. (1981). Occupational assimilation of refugees. *International Migration Review, 15*(1-2), 292-309.

Haines, D., Rutherford, D., & Thomas, P. (1981). Family and community among Vietnamese refugees. *International Migration Review, 15*(1-2), 510-519.

Hanh, P. (1979). The family in Vietnam and its social life. In J. Whitmore (Ed.), *An introduction to Indochinese history, culture, language, and life.* Ann Arbor: University of Michigan, Center for South and Southeast Asian Studies.

Hickey, G. (1964). *Village in Vietnam.* New Haven, CT: Yale Press.

Holmes, T., & Masuda, M. (1973). Life changes and illness susceptibility. In J. Scott & E. Senay (Eds.), *Separation and depression: Clinical and research aspects.* Washington, DC: American Association for the Advancement of Science.

Kelly, G. (1977). *From Vietnam to America: A chronicle of the Vietnamese immigration to the United States.* Boulder, CO: Westview Press.

Khoa, L. (1980). *Indochinese mutual assistance organizations as mechanisms in community mental health.* Paper presented at the National Conference on Social Welfare, 107th Annual Forum, Cleveland, OH.

Khoa, L., & Van Deusen, J. (1981). Social and cultural customs: Their contribution to resettlement. *Journal of Refugee Resettlement, 1*(2), 48-51.

Kinzie, J., & Manson, S. (1983). Five years' experience with Indochinese refugee psychiatric patients. *Journal of Operational Psychiatry, 14*(2), 105-111.

Kleinman, A. (1980). *Patients and healers in the context of culture.* Los Angeles: University of California Press.

Lin, E., Carter, W., & Kleinman, A. (1985). An exploration of somatization among Asian refugees and immigrants in primary care. *American Journal of Public Health, 75,* 1080-1084.

Lin, K., Masuda, M., & Tazuma, L. (1984). Problems of eastern refugees and immigrants: Adaptational problems of Vietnamese refugees, Part IV. *Psychiatric Journal of the University of Ottawa, 9,* 79-84.

Lin, K., Tazuma, L., & Masuda, M. (1979). Adaptational problems of Vietnamese refugees: I. Health and mental health status. *Archives of General Psychiatry, 36*, 955-961.

Liu, W., Lamanna, M., & Murata, A. (1979). *Transition to nowhere: Vietnamese refugees in America.* Nashville: Charter House.

Mamdani, M. (1973). *From citizen to refugee: Ugandans and Asians come to Britain.* London: Frances Pinter.

Marris, P. (1974). *Loss and change.* London: Routledge and Kegan Paul.

Marris, P. (1980). The uprootment of meaning. In G. Coelho & P. Ahmed (Eds.), *Uprooting and development* (pp.101-116). New York: Plenum Press.

Masuda, M., Lin, K., & Tazuma, L. (1980). Adaptational problems of Vietnamese refugees: II. Life changes and perceptions of life events. *Archives of General Psychiatry, 37,* 447-450.

Mathers, J. (1974). The gestation period of identity change. *British Journal of Psychiatry, 125,* 472-474.

Mattson, R., & Ky, D. (1978). Vietnamese refugee care: Psychiatric observations. *Minnesota Medicine, 61*(1), 33-36.

Meszaros, A. (1961). Types of displacement reactions among the post-revolution Hungarian immigrants. *Canadian Psychiatry Association Journal, 6,* 9-19.

Mokuau, N. (1987). Social workers' perceptions of counseling effectiveness for Asian-American clients. *Social Work, 32*(4), 331-335.

Montero, D. (1979). Vietnamese refugees in America: Toward a theory of spontaneous international migration. *International Migration Review, 13,* 624-648.

Park, R. (1928). Human migration and the marginal man. *American Journal of Sociology, 33,* 881-893.

Pennsylvania Department of Public Welfare. (1979). *National mental health needs assessment of Indochinese refugee populations.* Philadelphia Office of Mental Health, Bureau of Research and Training.

Pfister-Ammende, M. (1973). Mental hygiene in refugee camps. In C. Zwingmann & M. Pfister-Ammende (Eds.), *Uprooting and after.* New York: Springer.

Rahe, R., Looney, J., Ward, H., Tung, T., & Liu, W. (1978). Psychiatric consultation in a Vietnamese refugee camp. *American Journal of Psychiatry, 135,* 185-190.

Refugee Reports. (1985). Vol. 5. Nashville, TN: American Council for Nationalities Service.

Silver, B., & Chui, J. (1985). *Mental health issues: Indochinese refugees.* Rockville, MD: National Institute of Mental Health.

Smither, R., & Rodriguez-Giegling, M. (1979). Marginality, modernity and anxiety in Indochinese refugees. *Journal of Cross-Cultural Psychiatry, 10,* 469-478.

Stonequist, E. (1935). The problem of the marginal man. *American Journal of Sociology, 41*, 1-12.

Taft, J., North, D., & Ford, D. (1979). *Refugee resettlement in the US: Time for a new focus.* Washington, DC: New Trans-Century Foundation.

Tung, T. (1980). The Indochinese refugees as patients. *Journal of Refugee Resettlement, 1*(1), 53-60.

Tyhurst, L. (1971). Displacement and migration: A study in social psychiatry. *American Journal of Psychiatry, 107*, 561-568.

Tyhurst, L. (1981). *Coping with refugees: A Canadian experience, 1948-81.* Paper presented at the Seventh Annual SIETAR Conference, Vancouver, Canada.

Van Deusen, J. (1982). Health/mental health studies of Indochinese refugees: A critical overview. *Medical Anthropology, 6*, 231-252.

Van Deusen, J., et al. (1980). Southeast Asian social and cultural customs: Similarities and differences, Part I. *Journal of Refugee Resettlement, 1*(1), 53-60.

Zwingmann, C., & Pfister-Ammende, M. (1973). *Uprooting and after.* New York: Springer.

Chapter 7

Developing Effective Mental Health Policies and Services for Traumatized Refugee Patients
Richard F. Mollica

During the Year of the Snake, the God of the Sun came to stay in my body. It made my body shaky all over—and I fainted. Upon awakening, I can remember as I opened my eyes that it was very dark. I then went to the rice fields to find someone to ask them what time it was. A voice shouted ten o'clock. Suddenly, the owls began to cry and all the animals which represented death were howling all around me. I could also barely see a small group of people whispering to each other in the forest. I became so frightened that I tried to calm myself by praying to all the gods and the angels in heaven to protect me from danger. I was so paralyzed with fear that I was unable to walk either backwards or forwards.

I came to settle in East Boston near the ocean. Now when I dream, I always see an American who dresses in black walking along the sea. One day when I was in my sponsor's house, I had this vision. This year, the Year of the Cow, I would like the American people to help me build a temple which will be located near the seashore. Since the Pol Pot soldiers killed my children, I am so depressed that all I can think about is building a temple—that is all. God appeared to me again the other day, and he told me to build a temple. Please help me make my dream come true, if not, I do not think I can live any more.

This plea for help came to me from an elderly Cambodian widow who had lost her husband and most of her extended family during the Khmer Rouge regime (1975-79). This type of request for aid is certainly unfamiliar to most traditional mental health providers. However, since 1975, over one million Southeast Asian refugees have resettled in the United States *(Refugee Resettlement Program, 1984)*. Although many of these refugees experienced serious trauma and torture in their homeland, the American mental health establishment still struggles to provide appropriate services to those members of the refugee communities suffering from serious psychiatric disorders. Exceptions to this include not only the research and clinical efforts of our Boston group, the Indochinese Psychiatry Clinic (Science and the Citizen, 1985), but also the work of Kinzie and Manson (1983), Nguyen (1984), and Westermeyer, Vang, and Neider (1983). Recognizing that the clinical care of highly traumatized and tortured refugee patients is still in its infancy, this chapter presents an overview of the major public policy and clinical issues inherent in providing effective mental health services to Southeast Asian refugee communities.

Public Policy Barriers to Refugee Mental Health Care

The Impact of Language and Cultural Differences on Health-Seeking Behavior

The Indochinese refugee patient presents a special challenge to the health care provider. Aside from the obvious language barrier, cultural differences pose major problems as well. For example, Southeast Asians tend to feel that physical symptoms are the only legitimate reason to seek health care; they typically turn to folk healers and community resources (such as family members, Buddhist monks, or Catholic priests) for help with emotional problems. This behavior partly reflects Southeast Asians' widespread lack of familiarity with mental health practitioners and psychiatric institutions in their native countries, particularly in Laos and Cambodia. Moreover, a psychiatric diagnosis in the refugee camps is typically a severe impediment to immigration; thus an admission of mental illness or even of lesser psychological problems may be seen not only as a mark of weakness, but also as a threat to the refugee's new life in America. Yamamoto (1978) and Kinzie (1981) note that Asians are more likely than Westerners to feel humiliated by mental affliction and to expect ridicule therefrom. A standard of secretiveness therefore prevails that precludes sharing of the emotional upsets. In addition, refugees may be reluctant to discuss trauma-related events or symptoms with a health care practitioner because to do so raises painful feelings which the patients often would rather not relive.

High-Risk, Geographically Scattered Populations

From a mental health standpoint, refugees represent a high-risk, yet geographically scattered, population. State mental health systems lack the organizational structure to cope with them effectively. (State and local mental health programs have similar problems providing services to former mental patients who are homeless.) Neither centralized nor localized mental health facilities can effectively allocate resources for disabled individuals who require considerable care but who are few in number in any given geographical region. Moreover, Indochinese refugees do not all speak the same language.

In Massachusetts, for example, Indochinese refugees are distributed throughout the state, but only the Boston metropolitan area has a large enough concentration of Indochinese to justify the hiring of full-time clinicians speaking Cambodian, Hmong/Laotian, and Vietnamese (Science and the Citizen, 1985). The state has been financially unable to adequately serve areas of the state outside of Boston where significant (but relatively small) refugee populations reside. Because of the lack of Indochinese-speaking clinicians and support staff, refugee patients who are in need of psychiatric services, especially hospitalization, often languish for months in state mental hospitals before a team of experienced physicians and interpreters from a regional center (usually Boston) can provide on-site consultation. In states and regions where specialized programs do not exist (i.e., in the majority of states), refugee patients typically suffer from prolonged hospitalization in state mental hospitals, misdiagnosis, and limited treatment, if any.

Refugees as Public Patients

Refugee patients generally need publicly supported mental health care because of their limited economic resources. They represent a "new" population of public patients who are now competing with the traditional American minorities (i.e., Blacks and Hispanics) for a shrinking mental health dollar. Most state-supported mental health programs are experiencing serious fiscal cutbacks, resulting in a serious disintegration of publicly financed mental health care (Mollica, 1983). Refugee mental health specialists, like participants in other publicly supported programs, are therefore attempting to develop effective treatment models within an already resource-poor environment.

Refugees as "Low-Status" Patients

Numerous epidemiologic studies continue to reveal the applicability in American mental health facilities of Hollingshead and Redlich's (1958) original findings in *Social Class and Mental Illness*. This study demonstrated that lower-class patients received poorer care than those from higher socioeconomic backgrounds. Lower-class patients typically received brief treatment, usually consisting of custodial care and medication, from nonprofessional staff. Recent evidence continues to support the conclusion of Hollingshead and Redlich that social and cultural factors have a greater influence on the assignment of treatment (and quite possibly in the outcome of treatment) than symptoms or diagnosis (Mollica & Milic, 1986).

Refugee patients are a new category of low-status patient within the traditional hierarchy of client "attractiveness" that exists in American mental health. Thus, for example, many New England states have been unable to provide services to Indochinese patients for the past few years because they cannot find psychiatric and other mental health professionals willing to participate in refugee programs. The difficulty of recruitment will continue to hamper the development of refugee mental health care if and when state dollars become available for such specialized programs.

Clinical Barriers to Refugee Mental Health Services

American mental health care providers are generally unfamiliar with the various Indochinese culture-bound syndromes and the different attribution of meaning given symptoms by various cultures (Mollica, Wyshak, de Marneffe, Khuon, & Lavelle, 1987). For example, common American expressions such as "feeling blue" cannot be readily translated into Indochinese. A Cambodian clinician will ask Cambodian patients if they "feel blue" by using Cambodian terms which literally translate into "heavy, overcast, gloomy." The Laotian way of describing "feeling tense" is feeling like a "balloon blown up until it is about to burst." Westermeyer (1979, 1981), in a case-controlled study in Laos, furthermore documented the general inability of Western psychiatrists to recognize the Laotian symptoms of depression as well as to diagnose depression in Laotians who were suffering from a major affective disorder.

The trauma and torture experienced by many refugees are also unfamiliar to the majority of American practitioners (Mollica, Wyshak, & Lavelle, 1987). In spite of the numerous journalistic reports of the concentration camp experiences in Cambodia (Kiljunen, 1985), the sexual abuse of Vietnamese boat-women (U.S. Committee for Refugees, 1984), and the serious emotional distress associated with escape, refugee camp, and resettlement experiences, limited research exists on refugee trauma and trauma-related psychiatric disorders and social handicaps.

Even less is known concerning the most effective treatment for these problems. The field of psychiatric care of the traumatized and tortured is in its infancy (Goldfeld, Mollica, Pesavento, & Faraone, 1988). Information necessary to answer such basic questions as the following is simply not available: Are specialized torture centers more effective than general mental health programs? What is the best treatment for refugee trauma? Can native healers assist Western clinicians in treating tortured patients? Clearly, this lack of knowledge seriously impedes the development of effective treatment programs.

The Psychosocial Characteristics of
Indochinese Refugee Patients

This section summarizes the psychosocial characteristics of a treatment sample of 52 Indochinese patients treated by the Indochinese Psychiatry Clinic

(IPC) in 1984. These results have been presented in detail elsewhere (Mollica et al., 1985, 1987).

Trauma/Torture

Indochinese refugees primarily experienced severe trauma during three distinct periods: the war, their escape, and the refugee camps. Resettlement, although "psychologically traumatic," was not generally associated by IPC's patients with significant personal and physical injury.

The refugee's trauma experiences fell into four general categories:
1. deprivation (including lack of food, water, shelter, or medical attention;
2. physical injury/torture (including sexual abuse);
3. incarceration/reeducation camps (including solitary confinement and forcible separation from their children); and
4. witnessing the killing or torture of others.

Table 1

Mean Number of Trauma/Torture Events

	Trauma	Torture
Cambodian	16	3
Hmong/Laotian	11	1
Vietnamese	2	0

Table 1 shows the mean number of traumatic events experienced by IPC patients in Indochina. It reveals the high level of trauma and torture experienced by Cambodians as compared to other Indochinese groups. All the IPC patients in the study, however, had lived through serious multiple traumas. Not surprisingly, those patients diagnosed as suffering from post-traumatic stress disorder had experienced twice as many trauma events as those patients with other psychiatric diagnoses. Cambodian women who had lost their husbands (those who were separated, divorced, or widowed) had experienced the highest number of traumatic experiences as compared to all other clinical subgroups.

Family Support

Eighty percent of IPC's Cambodian patients stated they had no one (not even a family member) upon whom they could rely. This finding is dramatically different from the family support perceived by all other IPC patients. In contrast, Vietnamese and Laotian patients felt that they could obtain help with their emotional problems from their relatives.

Community Trust

More than 80 percent of the Cambodian patients perceived marked hostility and prejudice from Chinese and other Asians living in their community, while more than a third of them also felt prejudice and hostility from other Americans. In contrast, less than 10 percent of the Laotian and Vietnamese patients found Americans hostile and prejudiced against them.

Social Problems

IPC's Indochinese patients all indicated major difficulties with the triad of social needs identified by the U.S. Office of Refugee Resettlement—language, employment, and housing (Hawkes, 1983). Over 90 percent of IPC's patients cited language problems, and over 50 percent said employment and housing were major problems. Patients diagnosed as having post-traumatic stress disorder revealed twice as much discomfort in their housing situation as other patients. Spouseless Cambodian women (those widowed, separated, or divorced) had the lowest enrollment in ESL (English as a second language) classes. While most IPC refugee patients were actively attending such classes, only 55 percent of the spouseless Cambodian women were attending ESL classes.

Medical Disorders

Approximately 40 percent of the refugees of each nationality (Cambodian, Hmong/Laotion, and Vietnamese) were in need of ongoing medical treatment for medical disorders that included hepatitis, tuberculosis, leprosy, and heart disease.

Psychiatric Disorders

The major DSM-III diagnosis of IPC's 52 Indochinese patients was major affective disorder (71 percent). Other diagnoses included post-traumatic stress disorder (50 percent), schizophrenia (13 percent), and organic brain syndrome (8 percent). The majority of patients had more than one diagnosis.

Except for one case, the diagnosis of post-traumatic stress disorder (PTSD) was invariably associated with an additional psychiatric diagnosis, usually major affective disorder. Almost all patients diagnosed as having PTSD revealed a history of bad dreams and nightmares during the three major trauma periods (war, escape, and refugee camp). In addition, more than 90 percent of those patients with bad dreams and nightmares also experienced serious sleep disturbances. Patients with other diagnoses (and without PTSD) were less afflicted by bad dreams and nightmares (e.g., 62 percent of those diagnosed for a major affective disorder without PTSD had this symptom, as did 45 percent of all other diagnoses without PTSD).

Social Functioning

The majority of IPC's 52 patients had major social disabilities—85 percent functioned at a level of fair (DSM-III level 4) or poorer during the previous year. Only 22 percent of those patients with major affective disorder functioned at levels of good (level 3) to very good (level 2). Depressed patients who also had a diagnosis of PTSD functioned almost as well socially as those patients with only the diagnosis of major affective disorder.

Treatment Concerns

A comprehensive review of the psychiatric care of Indochinese refugee patients has been published elsewhere (Mollica & Lavelle, 1988). This section will highlight the major points in that review as well as the research findings described in the previous section, both of which are based upon IPC's clinical experience.

Evaluation and Diagnosis

Mental health providers who would treat refugee patients must be able to diagnose major affective disorder, post-traumatic stress disorder, organic brain syndrome, and schizophrenia. However, clinical diagnosis of refugee patients is difficult, not only because of cultural and linguistic barriers, but also because highly traumatized patients will avoid discussing their traumatic experiences and trauma-related symptoms. Getting refugee patients to provide details about their lives is often initially extremely difficult. On the other hand, it is not uncommon for refugee patients to begin their first evaluation interview with an extremely moving story (Cienfuegos & Monelli, 1983). In fact, it is extremely rare for refugee patients not to reveal "psychologically" minded details at some time during the course of their evaluation.

Clinicians should specifically ask Indochinese patients if they suffer from symptoms of post-traumatic stress disorder since the typical refugee patient will not freely mention these symptoms and in fact may initially deny them if asked. However, a history of nightmares and bad dreams often provides the only clinical evidence that patients have experienced serious trauma that they are emotionally ready to disclose (Kramer, Schoen, & Kinney, 1984). Moreover, it is not uncommon for the trauma event to be revealed in the telling of a dream (Van der Kolk, Blitz, Burr, Sherry, & Hartmann, 1984). It is not known, however, whether refugee patients meet all of the DSM-III criteria for post-traumatic stress disorder since some of the criteria such as "survival guilt" may be culture-bound symptoms (Horowitz, 1986; Kolb, 1984).

Duration and Intensity of Treatment

Highly traumatized refugee patients initially can tolerate only limited discussions of their lives. Moreover, scarce resources often make it impossible to provide each patient with a standard one-hour therapy session. Using a brief contact model, therapy must provide continuous weekly support of the patient. IPC's slogan—"A little, a lot, over a long period of time"—expresses the necessity of maintaining a long-term commitment to refugee patients. These patients need to know that they can continue to see their therapist indefinitely until their situation improves. A therapist's verbal commitment to long-term treatment is especially helpful to those refugees who are socially isolated or who feel hopeless about their ability to recover from the atrocities they have experienced.

The Indochinese Paraprofessional

Little cross-cultural literature exists on the relationship between patient, Western mental health professional, and bilingual interpreter (Borus et al., 1979). One senses, however, that Western professionals are not taking advantage of the knowledge of Southeast Asian paraprofessionals within this unique triad. This lack of appreciation of the cultural value of the bilingual interpreter is partially due to the hierarchical relationship that is assumed by Western health practitioners. Even within the most culturally sensitive medical settings, the interpreter is normally viewed simply as an aid to the diagnostic process.

This approach, however, is seriously flawed. Indochinese paraprofessionals are more than just interpreters or translators; they are specialized mental health clinicians who can conceptually move between Western models of disease and treatment and the unique medical and psychiatric world view of their own culture. A well-trained Indochinese clinician will convey subtle medical and cultural nuances between patient and physician. Yet most physicians and hospitals expect Indochinese clinicians to serve simply as the physician's personal mouthpiece (i.e., as an inanimate medical instrument or a telephone).

Psychopharmacology

Psychotropic drugs are widely used in the treatment of Indochinese refugee patients. Not only do these patients expect physicians to prescribe medications for their symptoms, but the severity of disorders that generally present to a refugee clinic demand that the treatment team be able to rapidly ameliorate the extreme psychological distress of their patients.

There is little research on transcultural psychopharmacology (Lin, Okamoto, Yamamoto, & Chien, 1986). Asians have been reported to be more likely to develop acute extrapyramidal side effects than whites on comparable doses of the tranquilizer haloperidol. Asians also appear to require lower doses of neuroleptics to achieve a therapeutic effect. Therefore, lower doses of most psychotropic medications can be used without compromising their therapeutic effect in Asians.

Kinzie, following Kolb (Boehnlein, Kinzie, Ben, & Fleck, 1985; Kramer et al., 1984), indicates the successful use of clonidine with patients suffering from PTSD. IPC has also successfully used parnate, the MAO-inhibitor, with refugee patients whose depressive symptoms failed to respond to standard tricyclics. All of the above observations, however, need to be validated by adequate drug trials.

Psychotherapy: The Key Role of the "Trauma Story"

The most effective form of therapy for victims of torture and the multiple traumas of mass violence is unknown (Genefke, 1984; Kinzie, Fredrickson, Ben, Fleck, & Karls, 1984). Traditional Western psychotherapy seems ill-prepared to address the degree of trauma experienced by many refugee patients (Kinzie et al., 1984). In addition, psychotherapy as practiced in the West is foreign both to Indochinese folk medicine practitioners and to Western-style Indochinese physicians. Yet, whatever the clinician's theoretical orientation, the "trauma story" emerges as the centerpiece of any treatment approach. Each and every refugee patient has at least one traumatic experience that figures prominently as an essential aspect of his or her life history. It is not uncommon for a refugee patient to respond to the question, "When did your problem begin?" by stating, "On April 20, 1975, at 6 p.m., the Communist troops. . ." The following two clinical vignettes from the Indochinese Psychiatry Clinic illustrate the centrality of the trauma story.

> **Case #1.** X. L. is a 40-year-old single Laotian female who was referred to IPC by the surgical unit at a general hospital following surgery for the treatment of active gall bladder disease. She developed disorganized thinking immediately following the surgical procedure, manifesting marked deterioration in social functioning, disorientation,

and paranoid ideation. She denied any prior psychiatric history, but stated, "I was probably crazy when I was a prisoner. They tortured me; they gave me many kinds of medicine that made me fly away. It made me forget what they did to me."

This patient was born in Laos to an affluent upper-class family. Her developmental history was reportedly normal. She attended private schools in both Laos and France, excelling in the study of languages (she speaks nine language fluently). As a young adult, she worked as a professor of languages until she was appointed to a prestigious political position which she held from 1971 until the Communist invasion in 1974 when her parents were assassinated and she became a war prisoner. X. L. states that she was tortured daily during her five years in captivity. She was also given mind-altering drugs and told they would eventually result in her death. X. L. states that she was raped each night by "20 to 30" guards. In 1979 she escaped to Thailand shortly after being transferred to a labor camp near the Laos-Thailand border. She eventually made her way to the United States in 1981. Bereft of relatives and friends, X. L. settled in the Boston area where she has had little contact with the Lao/Hmong community.

X. L.'s psychiatric treatment history since 1981 has included several admissions to community and state hospitals, as well as weekly outpatient therapy and psychopharmacological treatment. The patient's compliance has been inconsistent. Psychotic decompensations have occurred at least twice yearly. On a number of occasions, she has been found wandering and disoriented in cities in the United States and Canada, unaware of how she got there. Her frequent moves, which seem to be prompted by her fear of being recaptured by the Communists, have resulted in an inability to receive state disability benefits (she has not maintained a permanent address during her entire time in Boston). Her "homelessness" is exacerbated by her unstable mental status, and vice versa.

Case #2. C. C. is a 40-year-old Cambodian male with no past medical/psychiatric history. He was referred to IPC by a primary care clinic in January 1983, for an evaluation of depression since a medical basis could not be determined for his chronic headaches, dizziness, chest pain, blurred vision, and motion sickness.

C. C. was the fourth child born to a poor rural Cambodian family; his father was murdered when the patient was ten months old. Unable to educate C. C. or provide for his physical needs, the patient's mother gave him to a monk to serve as an apprentice at an area temple. He remained at the temple for ten years, then joined the army after the

Communist invasion. He was subsequently captured and escaped from a Communist prison four times. During one of his imprisonments, his mother suffered a fatal heart attack. His only sister died of starvation in his presence, after his frantic but futile attempts to find food for her.

C. C. has been married three times. He had three children and also raised his sister's son with whom he felt a special connection. The patient lost track of all the children during the war, and he does not know whether they died or remain alive. C. C. lives in the Boston area with his third wife (a marriage by the Pol Pot regime) and her 11-year-old daughter. Recently, a pregnancy from this union was terminated because of severe financial constraints upon the family.

C. C. presents with numerous somatic complaints, including headaches, chest pain, weakness, poor appetite, and motion sickness. C. C.'s depression is severe with major neurovegetative symptoms including severe psychomotor retardation, diminished appetite (resulting in a weight loss of 30 lbs.), and difficulty sleeping. One and a half years of treatment, including many drug trials, has resulted in only slight decreases in C. C.'s depressive symptoms.

Both of these patients have suffered horrific life experiences, but unfortunately they are not atypical. Many refugee patients have similar stories. The trauma story is a living reality and is always present for each patient. Yet, the story may be elusive and difficult for patient and therapist to share. Too often when the patient is ready to tell the trauma story, the clinician is not ready to hear it; then when the clinician is ready for the patient to tell his or her story, the patient may be unwilling. One of the major goals of psychotherapy for refugee patients, therefore, must be to allow the trauma story to gently emerge and become a familiar and acceptable theme within the clinic, and ultimately within the patient's family and community. This approach contradicts those who claim that hypnosis, abreaction, and catharsis can significantly reduce symptoms in trauma patients. These latter approaches have not proven useful with refugee patients—perhaps because the degree of trauma of refugee patients is so great or because these therapeutic devices are culturally inappropriate.

Despite the centrality of the trauma story, it is not clear that a retelling of the trauma story is in itself therapeutic. For many refugee patients, only limited revelation of their experiences can be tolerated since too much disclosure leads to serious and often unremitting psychic distress. Kinzie and his fellow researchers (1984), for example, found that, despite their creative attempts to therapeutically assist their patients with PTSD, the interview itself stimulated further intrusive thoughts, which intensified existing symptoms. There was no catharsis or healing effect from discussion of the past.

Nevertheless, the gentle sharing and acceptance of the trauma story (always at the patient's own pace and direction), although limited in its impact on symptom reduction, appears to significantly diminish the refugee patient's sense of shame, fear, and incompetence. It helps the patients give meaning to their questions: "Why did this happen to me? How can human beings be so cruel?" More often than not, refugee patients find that family members, members of their own community, and other Americans do not welcome their stories. In fact, many health practitioners also shy away from hearing these tragic life histories (Haley, 1974).

The trauma story, then, can help the clinician bridge the disrupted social connection that exists between patients and their families and community. Many of IPC's refugee patients are seriously depressed, and most also experience many trauma-related symptoms including frequent nightmares (in which they relive the trauma events) and bad dreams and memories. Patients sometimes describe these symptoms as engulfing them in a living hell. These patients live in a world of traumatic images and memories in which nothing else exists for them except the trauma story. Their psychological reality is paradoxically both full and empty. They are full of the past, but largely empty of new ideas and life experiences. Social isolation and impaired social functioning are also present. As the refugee patient's distress intensifies, the patient may be abandoned by his or her friends and relatives.

Thus, the clinical staff is often the only social contact of traumatized refugee patients. Yet, maintaining this contact is difficult because of the general lack of trust these patients have in any individual who lives in a world that has generated for them so much cruelty. Although the trauma story is an inner personal obsession, it may take years before patients will share their life history with their clinicians. IPC's staff members have found that the bridging of disrupted social connections can lead patients to a more realistic assessment of their present reality—a reality that can be shared with their family, friends, and community.

Conclusion

Imagine now a man who is deprived of everyone he loves and, at the same time, of his house, his habits, his clothes, in short, of everything he possesses: he will be a hollow man, reduced to suffering and needs, forgetful of dignity and restraint, for he who loses all often easily loses himself. He will be a man whose life or death can be lightly decided with no sense of human affinity, in the most fortunate of cases, on the basis of a pure judgment of utility. It is in this way that one can understand the double sense of the term "extermination camp," and it is now clear what we seek to express with the phrase: "to lie on the bottom" (Levi, 1985, p. 27).

This chapter has briefly reviewed some of the major public policy and clinical issues that impinge on the development of mental health services to refugee patients. Of course, many other considerations (such as the inadequacy of public financing) are also relevant. Is there any hope that effective, culturally sensitive programs for refugees will eventually emerge despite nonexistent state and federally supported mental health programs, limited clinical and research experience, and the serious decline of publicly supported mental health care? Normal human beings (including mental health professionals) shrink away from confronting the refugee's hopelessness and despair. Yet, these silent sufferers need to be heard and, like the survivors of the Jewish holocaust, will eventually be heard as they rise up from the "bottom."

Note: This chapter is based on data originally presented at the National Institute of Mental Health's workshop on "Long-Term Effects of Mass Violence: Cross-Cultural Treatment and Research Issues in Post-Traumatic Stress Disorder, April 14-15, 1986.

References

Boehnlein, J. K., Kinzie, J. D., Ben, R., & Fleck, J. (1985). One-year follow-up study of post-traumatic stress disorder among survivors of Cambodian concentration camps. *American Journal of Psychiatry, 142,* 956-959.

Borus, J. F., Anastasi, M., Casoni, R., Dello Russo, R., Dimascio, L., Fusco, L., Rubenstein, J., & Snyder, M. (1979). Psychotherapy in the goldfish bowl: The role of the indigenous therapist. *Archives of General Psychiatry, 36,* 187-190.

Cienfuegos, A. J., & Monelli, C. (1983). The testimony of political repression as a therapeutic instrument. *American Journal of Orthopsychiatry, 53,* 43-51.

Genefke, I. K. (1984, September). *Rehabilitation of torture victims.* Paper presented at the Conference on the Violation of Human Rights, Beverly Hills, CA.

Goldfeld, A., Mollica, R. F., Pesavento, B., & Faraone, S. (1988). The physical and psychological sequelae of torture: Symptomatology and diagnosis. *Journal of the American Medical Association, 259*(18), 2725-2729.

Haley, S. (1974). When the patient reports atrocities: Specific treatment considerations of the Vietnam veteran. *Archives of General Psychiatry, 30,* 191-196.

Hawkes, P. (1983). A review of the refugee program in the United States. Office of Refugee Resettlement, *Proceedings of the Southeast Asian Mental Health in the Western Context: Grief Process, Disaster, Reaction, Cultural Conflict,* (pp. 50-54).

Hollingshead, A. B., & Redlich, F. C. (1958). *Social class and mental illness.* New York: John Wiley & Sons.

Horowitz, M. J. (1986). Stress-response syndromes: A review of post-traumatic and adjustment disorders. *Hospital & Community Psychiatry, 37,* 241-249.

Kiljunen, K. (1985). Power politics and the tragedy of Kampuchea during the seventies. *Bulletin of Concerned Asian Scholars, 17,* 49-64.

Kinzie, J. D. (1981). Evaluation and psychotherapy of Indochinese refugee patients. *American Journal of Psychiatry, 35,* 251-261.

Kinzie, J. D., Fredrickson, R. B., Ben, R., Fleck, J., & Karls, W. (1984). Post-traumatic stress disorder among survivors of Cambodian concentration camps. *American Journal of Psychiatry, 141,* 645-650.

Kinzie, J. D., & Manson, S. (1983) Five years' experience with Indochinese refugee psychiatric patients. *Journal of Operational Psychiatry, 14,* 105-111.

Kolb, L. C. (1984). The post-traumatic stress disorder of combat: A subgroup with a conditioned emotional response. *Military Medicine, 149,* 237-243.

Kramer, M., Schoen, L. S., & Kinney, L. (1984). Long-term effects of traumatic stress. In B. A. Van der Kolk (Ed.), *Adult psychic trauma: Psychological and physiological sequelae* (pp. 51-96). Washington, DC: American Psychiatric Press.

Levi, P. (1985). *Survival in Auschwitz and the reawakening.* New York: Summit Books.

Lin, K. M., Okamoto, T., Yamamoto, J., & Chien, C. P. (1986). Psychotropic dosage in Asian patients. *P/AAMHRC Research Review, 5,* 1-16.

Mollica, R. F. (1983). From asylum to community: The threatened disintegration of public psychiatry. *New England Journal of Medicine, 308,* 367-373.

Mollica, R. F., & Lavelle, J. (1988). Southeast Asian refugee. In L. Comas-Díaz & E. H. Griffith (Eds.), *Clinical issues in cross-cultural mental health.* New York: John Wiley & Sons.

Mollica, R. F., & Milic, M. (1986). Social class and psychiatric practice: A revision of the Hollingshead and Redlich model. *American Journal of Psychiatry, 143,* 12-17.

Mollica, R. F., Wyshak, G., Coelho, R., & Lavelle, J. (1985). *The Southeast Asian psychiatry patient: A treatment outcome study.* Washington, DC: U.S. Office of Refugee Resettlement.

Mollica, R. F., Wyshak, G., de Marneffe, D., Khuon, F., & Lavelle, J. (1987). Indochinese versions of the Hopkins Symptom Checklist-25: A screening instrument for the psychiatric care of refugees. *American Journal of Psychiatry, 144,* 497-500.

Mollica, R. F., Wyshak, G., & Lavelle, J. (1987). The psychosocial impact of war trauma and torture on Southeast Asian refugees. *American Journal of Psychiatry, 144,* 1567-1572.

Nguyen, S. D. (1984). Mental health services for refugees and immigrants. *Psychiatric Journal of the Ottawa University, 9,* 85-91.

Refugee Resettlement Program. (1984). Report to Congress, January 31, 1984—U.S. Department of Social Service Administration, Office of Refugee Resettlement. Washington, DC: U.S. Government Printing Office.

Science and the Citizen. (1985, July). *Scientific American,* pp. 58, 60.

U.S. Committee for Refugees. (1984). *Vietnamese boat people: Pirates' vulnerable prey.* Washington, DC: American Council for Nationalities Service.

Van der Kolk, B., Blitz, R., Burr, W., Sherry, S., & Hartmann, E. (1984). Nightmares and trauma: A comparison of nightmares after combat with lifelong nightmares in veterans. *American Journal of Psychiatry, 141,* 187-190.

Westermeyer, J. (1979). Folk concepts of mental disorder among the Lao: Continues with similar concepts in other cultures and in psychiatry. *Culture, Medicine, & Psychiatry, 3,* 301-317.

Westermeyer, J. (1981). Lao folk diagnoses for mental disorder: Comparison with psychiatric diagnosis and assessment with psychiatric rating scales. *Medical Anthropology, 5,* 425-443.

Westermeyer, J., Vang, T. F., & Neider, J. (1983). A comparison of refugees using and not using a psychiatric service: An analysis of DSM-III criteria and self-rating scales in cross–cultural context. *Journal of Operational Psychiatry, 14,* 36-40.

Yamamoto, J. (1978). Therapy for Asian Americans. *Journal of the National Medical Association, 70,* 267-270.

Part Three

Working with Sojourners

Chapter 8

Intercultural Adjustment
of Families Living Abroad

Sandra Mumford Fowler and Fanchon Silberstein

Counselors and trainers who work with families to prepare them for the challenges of overseas living readily observe that some families are more spontaneous than others in the clinical or training setting. These families often seem more open to new experiences and to exploring the unknown. They tend to quickly establish rapport with professionals and to react to new concepts with questions rather than hostility Such qualities of openness, perceiving the unknown as a challenge rather than a threat, interacting easily with strangers, and seeking ways to solve problems are indicators of an ability to function effectively in a new culture. Because mental health researchers who observe families in settings other than training situations note that these same qualities generally characterize healthy families, we conclude that descriptors of family health and intercultural effectiveness share many of the same characteristics.

W. Robert Beavers, in *Psychotherapy and Growth: A Family Systems Perspective* (1977), describes optimal families by applying a model he developed during a six-year study with Jerry Lewis at the Timberlawn Foundation in Dallas, TX. We find that the eight characteristics they identified equate with those of families who appear to function well when faced with intercultural challenges. A counselor or trainer who is familiar with the Beavers model can use it to observe and identify healthy family functioning and to reinforce these characteristics. Furthermore, a professional who is working with families that are less than optimal can help those families move toward the healthy behavior described by the eight characteristics of the model.

This chapter reviews selected literature on families and stress, describes the Beavers model, outlines components of effective intercultural preparation for relocating families, and emphasizes the value of reinforcing adaptive behavior to facilitate intercultural learning and adjustment. Because Beavers studied families from the United States, some of the characteristics in his model may not apply to families from other cultures. Nevertheless, we believe that certain components of effective intercultural training do carry across cultures and that our central idea—that a trainer or counselor can effectively reinforce qualities of intercultural effectiveness by referring to a model of healthy functioning—will prove useful to trainers and counselors in all cultures. We also recognize that the gender of family members may directly influence their perceptions of another culture and their inclusion in the life of that culture. Because the ability to adapt to a culture's specific attitudes toward males and females is one of the challenges that relocating families face, this should be handled in training and counseling when appropriate.

In this chapter we describe family health in functional terms. Our intent is to use Beavers' terminology to illustrate the ways adaptive families behave, not to attach labels to these families. Consequently, "health" is indicated by specific actions or categories of behaviors.

Following a review of the literature, we look at the particular tasks and stresses that a relocating family faces and connect these to counseling and training design.

Review of the Literature

The difficulties and challenges of family adjustment and the key role that family adjustment plays in professional performance were recognized in the literature in the mid-1960s, when researchers began reporting mental health considerations of family adaptation overseas. A body of literature existed that focused on such topics as selection and training of overseas personnel (e.g., Guthrie & McKendry, 1964; Torre, 1963), evaluating personnel and programs overseas (Golin, 1963), and the art of overseasmanship (Cleveland & Mangone, 1957).

David and Elkind (1966) were among the first to recognize that personal performance abroad was impacted by family interrelationships. Bower (1967) observed that severe mental illnesses were not the critical problem in the average American military community overseas, but rather that small problems festered and simple irritations became complex. Since culture shock is a real and significant fact for overseas families, Bower concluded that prevention of emotionally disabling and ineffective living is a necessary public health measure.

The 1970s produced a sizable amount of work in the area of family stress, yielding new substantive findings and extensions of already existing models and theory (McCubbin et al., 1980). Although the field has advanced its understanding of family dynamics, family stress, and coping, very few mental health models are being applied specifically to the dynamics of families undergoing the stress of relocation to a foreign environment.

Stress resulting from intercultural transition is somewhat unique. According to Rigamer (1985), "For the professional caring for people who live abroad, there are probably few other occasions when it is more important to evaluate a presenting problem in the context of the individual's life circumstances" (p. 137). Rigamer's list of stressors includes the move itself, objections by family members to relocation, adapting to a new culture, learning the language, and terrorism.

In a classic guide to bringing up children overseas, Werkman (1977) concluded that a family unit suffers total disruption with an overseas move when social and emotional supports are no longer available. He claims that an overseas move may "exact a heavy toll of suffering unless all members of a family work at making their adjustment a successful one" (p. 57).

Culture-shock-related stress assaults an individual's psychological and physiological systems (Adler, 1986; Barna, 1983; Copeland & Griggs, 1985; Grove & Torbiorn, 1985; Torbiorn, 1982; Weaver, 1986). Piet-Pelon and Hornby (1985) list various signs of stress due to culture shock: inability to concentrate, altered sleep patterns, physical illness, withdrawal or denial, marital problems, and depression. Culture shock reactions can range from mild emotional disorders and stress-related physical problems to full-blown psychoses (Weaver, 1986). Adler (1986) reports that stress-related culture shock may take many forms such as "embarrassment, disappointment, frustration, impatience, anxiety, identity problems, anger, and physiological problems such as sleeplessness, stomachaches, and trembling hands" (p.195).

It stands to reason that if any or all of these reactions are affecting individual family members, the entire family system is disrupted and it must marshall its energy and resources to overcome the difficulties. Moreover, this is happening at a time when family members' individual resources are at a low ebb. According to Fowler (1985), "A family's coping resources are especially challenged by an overseas assignment. The problems that lead to the difficulties and disorientation experienced upon arrival overseas are all manageable by themselves. But in combination they can feel overwhelming" (p. 1).

The ability of the family to cope with culture shock is critical. A husband and wife are very dependent on one another for support while experiencing culture shock (Torbiorn, 1982). Survey results (Gurin, 1985) show that the family is the primary agent of personal change and the most effective energy source to get people unstuck from unhealthy habits and help members live at their best.

Researchers have become increasingly convinced that studying healthy families is essential (Kaslow, 1981; Oliveri, 1982). In her search for a conceptualization of healthy and fulfilling functioning, Kaslow (1981) found that, among others, the Beavers-Timberlawn model was a valuable assessment tool for families that appeared clinically healthy to her (p. 11).

Trainers are most apt to meet relocating families in the orientation or preparation stage, where, through intercultural programs, they prepare specific groups to reside in specific target cultures for specific purposes (Paige, 1986). The outcome of an effective training program can be seen as inoculation to stress, "potentiating new skills, enhancing feelings of self-efficacy, self-confidence, hope, perceived control, commitment and personal responsibility" (Meichenbaum, 1985, p. 17).

Wallach and Metcalf (1981) describe living overseas as both an opportunity and a challenge to families. This chapter will present a model of a healthy family which will help families realize the opportunities inherent in an intercultural transition.

Components of an Orientation Program

In preparing families for an overseas relocation, a trainer or counselor must recognize that the relocation itself is a major event, one that will create considerable stress and require families to mobilize skills they may not have previously exercised. A family, by virtue of the varying ages of its members, its developmental needs, and perceptions of what a move will mean, is not inherently designed to be a strong problem-solving group. Unlike a typical working body in an organization, mothers, fathers, and children are not trained to organize material items, deal with economic matters, attend meetings, or coordinate the services of others. Yet a relocating family must carry out a myriad of tasks at the same time that it is dealing with physical and emotional stress affecting everything from diet and sleep patterns to interpersonal relationships. In addition, to manage any multifaceted task effectively, members of a group must negotiate and communicate effectively among themselves. While many families have these skills and exercise them as a matter of course, others are likely to be deficient in some areas. Counselors and trainers need to recognize that teaching and reinforcing good communication skills are an essential aspect of preparation for overseas relocation.

The design of a training or orientation program for overseas relocation should include at least three components:

1. *Each member of the family must be considered in the counselor's selection of content, activities, materials, and timing of training.* Family makeup, the ages of each member, their previous experience with relocation, their educational needs and levels, and career stages are some of the issues that the program designer should consider. Younger children, for example, are more responsive to interactive exercises and to materials they can manipulate. Adolescents often benefit more from peer counseling. Spouses may require an examination of role changes in leaving a career behind or becoming a full-time parent in a new cultural milieu. A discussion of normal adjustment patterns and adjustment techniques may relieve an employee of some worries about relocating a family. The training or counseling room needs to contain suitable props such as writing and drawing paper, pens and pencils, masking tape, movable chairs, and snacks. The length of particular exercises and the timing of breaks will vary according to the ages and needs of the family members.

2. *Exercises should reinforce healthy family functioning.* Variables identified by Beavers (1977) model in healthy family functioning provide the

foundation for identifying a family's problem-solving ability in the face of a challenging relocation. Most families will display some of these characteristics, and a counselor can help them to develop others. Reminding families of their existing skills and strengths helps reinforce their hope and confidence.

3. *The emphasis should be on promoting intercultural learning and adjustment that will continue beyond the counseling or training setting.* Effective intercultural training provides methods for dealing with family members' fears and expectations, cultural adjustment, communication styles within the family, and culture-specific information. With better self-understanding and increased insight into new situations, as well as specific methods for gaining information, families should be better prepared and better able to manage the initial adaptation and to continue their intercultural learning. Although the exercises in this chapter may seem more appropriate for a training than a counseling setting, many of them derive from clinical practice. Clinicians use these and other exercises in family sessions to give families opportunities to practice new skills, while trainers use these same kinds of exercises in workshops and seminars.

The Optimal Family: The Beavers Model

As noted earlier, Beavers (1977) conducted a systems-oriented project in which he observed the functioning of a number of families over a six-year period. This research resulted in the ordering of families along a continuum with respect to their flexibility, adaptability, and goal achievement. Beavers found that individual and family competence fluctuated depending upon their ability to solve problems presented by internal and external stresses occurring at various developmental periods. Observers watched families performing tasks and measured these families according to various criteria: structure, mythology, goal-directed negotiation, system tolerance for autonomy, and affect or feeling issues.

Structure concerns the way in which power is distributed within a family. Beavers found that competent individuals negotiate from positions of shared, overt power and do not rely either on intimidation or helplessness. Other aspects of structure are the parental coalition (did parents lead together or compete?) and family closeness—with the continuum ranging from true intimacy to no communication among family members.

Mythology describes the accuracy of the family members' assessment of the family. Beavers found that the healthiest families describe themselves very much as an outside observer would.

Goal-directed negotiation describes a family's efficiency in problem solving.

System tolerance for autonomy involves clarity of communication and the ability to express subjective feelings comfortably. Families who cannot tolerate directness tend to resort to obscure modes of communicating information about themselves. Autonomy also refers to the degree to which individuals assume personal responsibility for their expression and behavior. Healthier families encourage this while less competent families tend to resort to denial and blame to avoid responsibility. Furthermore, competent families do not attempt to mind-read and thereby negate individual members' thoughts and feelings. On the contrary, they are receptive to communication from one another, even from the youngest family members, and through their receptiveness, encourage the development of each member's dignity and self-esteem.

Affect or feeling issues are concerned with allowing or encouraging expression of feelings. The tone of a family may be either warm or cool. The degree of conflict and the amount of empathy between family members also vary. Conflict is inevitable in any family; it is the ability to resolve conflict that distinguishes healthy families from those that are less healthy or dysfunctional.

In Beavers' Timberlawn study, the research focused on family functioning, on systems, and on human interaction rather than on pathology and isolated individuals. The researchers, in seeking a definition of a healthy family, ultimately identified health as a process of growth, adaptation, and change. In doing so, they rejected the definition that labels health as the absence of emotional illness and those definitions that depend on a statistical average since this would mean that very healthy families (what they termed optimal) would be seen as deviant. They did not define normality as optimal functioning determined by a theoretical system since that could lead to an all-good or all-bad approach within the system.

The research yielded eight variables that Beavers identified as characterizing an optimal, or very healthy, family. While relatively few families are optimal, nearly all have some optimal characteristics. A counselor or trainer can help families identify their optimal qualities and reinforce them during the period of preparation for a move to a new culture. This helps families see where their problem-solving abilities lie and how these can work for them in meeting intercultural challenges. The eight characteristics identified by Beavers are identified as Table 1.

Systems Orientation

Families with a systems orientation realize that individuals need a group and that human life is interpersonal. They see that maturity involves the evolution of new relationships over time and the development of skills for meeting their own and others' needs in groups in which they participate. Their rules are compatible with, but not necessarily the same as, those of society.

Healthy families also see causes and effects as interchangeable. They know, for example, that hostility in one person promotes deception in others, and that deception in turn promotes hostility. Without this understanding, families frequently become confused, looking for simple causes for frustration and retreating to vague answers invoking fate or destiny.

Table 1

Characteristics of Optimal Families

1. A systems orientation inclusive of four assumptions:
   o   Any individual needs a group.
   o   Causes and effects are interchangeable.
   o   Behavior results from many variables.
   o   All human beings have limitations.
2. Healthy boundaries
3. Contextual clarity
4. Power balance
5. Encouragement of autonomy
6. Appropriate display of affect
7. Negotiation and task efficiency
8. Transcendent values

Healthy families know that many variables influence behavior. The task of relocating may seem overwhelming, but these families realize that work done in one area to counteract one deficiency affects others. Consequently, their attitude toward predeparture training is likely to be positive since they appreciate the usefulness of acquiring even small skills.

Healthy families accept the normal limitations of human beings. They know that self-esteem lies in competence rather than omnipotence and that negotiation with others is essential. Consequently, they can face risks in cross-culture challenges without exaggerating the effects of a possible mistake. They know that an error does not in itself represent failure. Similarly, they tend to be tolerant of new acquaintances and accepting of their limitations. Because they realize that other people do not exist to gratify their needs, they are less likely to interpret as hostile foreign behavior that makes them uncomfortable.

Healthy Boundaries

Beavers uses the analogy of a cell to illustrate the external boundary of a healthy family. Both possess enough strength and integrity to allow effective interchange within their borders. Thus, the optimal family gets and uses new information and discards old patterns that are no longer useful. A healthy family that is living abroad temporarily will maintain its rituals, knowing that this builds pride in the family and a sense of closeness. For example, at Christmas-time a family that is living in the tropics might hang familiar ornaments on an artificial evergreen tree (or even a coconut palm). Their holiday food and the gifts they exchange will not be what they would have been at home, and they will miss some of the familiar events of the season, but they nevertheless commemorate the holiday as a family and include new acquaintances in their celebration. A family lacking strength and integrity might observe their holiday alone, importing all of their gifts from home and attempting to ignore their relocation as a factor in their celebration. Or they might choose not to celebrate at all because they cannot maintain their old patterns in the same familiar form.

Contextual Clarity

This term describes a family in which there are clear roles and expectations. The expectations are realistic, and children are not expected to live out parental fantasies. Relocating families generally find that children are more adept than adult members at moving out into a new cultural milieu. Children often learn a foreign language more easily, make friends at school, and accept less critically the benefits and limitations of living in a new location. This adaptability is often difficult for families because it creates a power imbalance where the parents are not the leaders. Instead, the youngest member of the family may be the most adept. The healthy family will accept this, realizing that although they may feel somewhat threatened by what feels like a defection, they can appreciate that in the time and place in which they are living, the child is adapting well and that their own behaviors and expectations may need to shift. This necessitates a strong parental coalition, the starting point for contextual clarity, in which parents share overt power.

When contextual issues are clear, family members do not engage in stereotyping that denies human complexity. They can accept a wide range of feelings and perceptions among themselves and others, and they can understand that rules may shift as a situation requires. For example, at home, a family may expect its teenagers to help serve food at adult parties; if, however, this is determined to be unseemly behavior by families in their adopted country, the family would drop this requirement in deference to their new context. Because roles and expectations continue to be clear, they can drop a specific behavior without threatening the overall family structure.

Power Balance

In healthy families, there are few self-defeating power struggles. As we have seen, specific situations determine who has the greater influence, and children contribute actively while parents lead with an egalitarian coalition.

The demands of a move often require parents to become very directive so that the organizing, packing, and numerous other tasks may be dispatched. There is a place for authoritarian control; when used effectively, it can allow the family under pressure to accomplish a great deal. At the same time, younger members of the family need to have input. Competent parents give children time for their separate good-byes to friends. Each child packs his or her own suitcase with treasured items not necessarily considered essential to anyone else. In general, the family undertakes tasks with good-humored effectiveness, and when they do express anger, they do so openly and direct it more toward a goal or behavior than toward a person. In learning a new language, for example, they express distress over their own individual frustration, or they sympathize with another's difficulty by noting how tough it is, not by calling the learner slow or stupid.

Encouragement of Autonomy

Autonomous people are aware of their thoughts and feelings and take responsibility for their behavior. While this encourages flexibility and adaptability and discourages stereotyped roles, healthy families nevertheless hold strong loyalties and beliefs as part of their identities. Not all beliefs are open to negotiation.

A foreign environment might result in families accepting certain activities that are deemed inappropriate at home or prohibiting other activities that would be normal at home. For example, a child who, at home, is thought to be too young to use public transportation alone, may be allowed to move about freely in a European city to go to school or visit friends. In the same city, the family teenager may not be allowed to drive an automobile at an age when Americans would typically receive their license. The teenager accepts, though not without some frustration, the fact that teenage emancipation and maturity are tied to more than a driver's license.

Overall, autonomy implies a coherent expression of views and feelings and the ability to tell the truth without fear of punishment. Members of optimal families can handle ambivalence, and parents and children can fail without losing face or being defined as inadequate.

Appropriate Display of Affect

Healthy families tend to be warm, optimistic, and intense. Relocating families may feel their own lack of affect when outside connections are disrupted and they are thrown back on themselves. Many needs and desires of family members may not be met at any given time, but at home, in a familiar country, a family has more resources than are readily available in a new culture. Family members, particularly during a move and upon arrival in a new situation, need to depend upon one another more than usual for warmth, reassurance, and understanding.

A family that is relocating may have very high expectations for its members. The typical executive family that goes abroad expects that the employee will work to top efficiency, that the spouse will become a prized member of the expatriate community, that the children will be better human beings because of this formative experience, and that they will all learn the language and cultivate a wide circle of international friends. In reality, a healthy family recognizes that its wishes may reach beyond its ability to perform and can work constructively with a counselor to set priorities and test their capabilities slowly. Their understanding that human relationships are too complex for simple responses helps them; and this extends to their new intercultural relationships. They can approach these new relationships expecting satisfying encounters at the same time that they realize that they live in an imperfect world in which relationships are never totally rewarding. They can accept and savor friendships even where communication and understanding are limited.

Finally, when conflict arises within the family, healthy individuals tend to respond appropriately and immediately, thereby precluding resentment. A counselor can help a family appreciate the value of such responsiveness, yet forewarn them that there are likely to be many intercultural situations where an immediate response could cause misunderstanding. Competent family members are sensitive to assessing the feelings of others through a synthesis of voice, verbal context, and communication patterns and can be encouraged to use that sensitivity to observe and assess others in a new cultural context.

Negotiation and Task Efficiency

Healthy families have the capacity to accept directions, organize themselves to respond to a task, develop input from other members, negotiate differences, and provide clear, effective responses to a challenge. Seeing group goals as compatible with individual goals enables them to resolve conflicts. When one member of the family is successful, all share a sense of pride or pleasure in that success.

An intercultural move presents both large and small challenges and often calls for new behaviors. For example, if the family moves into a traditional culture where it is considered rude for a young child to enter a room and not greet elders separately, a child will be called upon to do this. Children exercise the new behavior because of the new context, knowing that they are contributing to the family's pride in adapting to a cultural requirement.

Transcendent Values

The ability of family members to adapt to the inevitable losses associated with growth and development, aging and death underlies all the family systems variables discussed thus far. Values are clear in optimal families, but they are expressed more through everyday transactions and processes than in a precisely verbalized set of beliefs. Family values nearly always emerge in relocation training sessions, and a counselor can highlight these as an affirmation of the family as a cohesive unit. When healthy families face change, they naturally draw support from the values and beliefs that underlie their behavior and hence tend to be less frightened of the unknown. Most families must give up some prized possessions when they move—be it friends, a pet, a school, or a familiar house. This can lead to strong feelings of loss and resentment. A healthy family can recognize the legitimacy of such feelings but will also accept a counselor's encouragement to look forward to activities, friends, and new experiences they could not have enjoyed at home.

A Framework for Promoting
Intercultural Learning and Adjustment

Now that a conceptual base has been established for identifying adaptive and maladaptive family systems and behaviors, it is time to consider effective intercultural preparation and training exercises. These are designed to promote intercultural learning and adjustment and to allow specific, rather than random, reinforcement of the behaviors that characterize well-functioning family systems. The exercises described below can be used in either a training or a clinical setting. Many of them can be conducted effectively with a single family, whereas others require several families. With some modifications, all the exercises can be used with individuals that are not part of a family group. Most of the exercises can be conducted effectively either prior to departure or upon arrival in the foreign country. It is not the purpose of this chapter to describe the exercises in extensive detail. Rather, the suggestions should spark ideas about new ways to work with families or reinforce techniques currently being used.

The framework used for intercultural preparation is perhaps more important than the exercises themselves. This framework consists of four elements: (a) fears and expectations, (b) cultural adjustment, (c) communication, and (d) culture-specific information. Any preparation program or relocation counseling should attend to each of these core components. In the remainder of the chapter, each core component of intercultural preparation is discussed and examples of exercises cited to illustrate how the exercises and the Beavers model can be integrated to enhance the preparation of the family.

Fears and Expectations

It is not at all unusual to experience some degree of fear or anxiety about living in a foreign environment. However, some families become paralyzed and overwhelmed by all the issues they are trying to handle prior to a move.

For example, in working with a relocation counselor before moving to Botswana, the Smith family—John and Martha and their seven-year-old son, Johnny, and thirteen-year-old daughter, Susie—clearly needed to work out their many fears. The counselor asked each of them to draw one fear about moving overseas. Johnny, who had not talked much, immediately drew their cat, Cocoa, on her back, all four paws in the air. In the ensuing tearful discussion, his fears about Cocoa not being able to survive the move to Botswana emerged. Gentle questioning revealed that talk at home about inoculations had made Johnny fearful, not just about Cocoa, but that the whole family, and especially Mother, might die. The other family members reassured Johnny that the family would continue to take care of one another in Botswana just as in the United States and that discussions of inoculations and diseases did not mean that they would get sick. At the end of the session, the counselor turned the picture of Cocoa upside down so that her paws were firmly on the ground, and Johnny was smiling again.

Three variations of this exercise are as follows: (a) ask the family members to draw a combined picture of their fears, (b) ask each member of the family to draw his or her own fear, and (c) develop a family "sculpture" that expresses a shared fear. This exercise is then processed to help family members see what they can do about their fears and how they can help each other. This provides an opportunity for family members to talk about issues that they might not ordinarily deal with and to achieve a perspective on emotionally laden concerns.

Expectations are one of the most powerful predictors of adjustment. Positive, realistic expectations pave the way for successful transition. Either a positive or a negative preliminary appraisal establishes a mind-set that will be selectively reinforced. Consequently, families living abroad will interpret events in the host country either positively or negatively depending on their mind-set. For example, if a person with negative expectations should get lost, it may be construed as a terrible event to be blamed on those people who don't speak English. For someone with positive expectations, getting lost would likely be viewed as an adventure and the source of a great story. A trainer or clinician can assist the formation of positive, yet realistic, expectations by using questions such as, "What do you most hope will happen?" or statements such as "I will feel successful if (fill in the blank)." The family members' responses need to be processed for realism and, if negative, reframed.

These types of exercises create many opportunities to encourage various aspects of optimal family functioning such as autonomy and negotiation, resolution of power issues, and development of contextual clarity. As was seen with the example of the Smith family, they may also create opportunities to reinforce affect, task efficiency, and the systems orientation of a family.

Cultural Adjustment

Counseling or training sessions can be built around understanding culture shock and cultural adjustment. This is important since the intercultural experience is likely to change family members in deep and subtle ways. In their everyday lives, they may be too busy to concentrate on such changes but it has been found that when people learn about adjusting, they can manage the process better. *BaFa BaFa* (Shirts, 1973) is a classic simulation game designed to help people understand many of the elements of entering another culture. In the span of just a few hours, participants experience some of the emotions, frustrations, and cognitive challenges of cultural differences, cultural "baggage," stereotypes, language barriers, and values conflicts. This game, in which two cultures are created and cross-cultural visits take place, works as well for people who have never been overseas as for those who have. The game requires 12 to 30 people to play, plus two rooms and at least two hours. A children's version, *RaFa RaFa*, is also available.

A family wrote their counselor, "Our BaFa experience began the minute we stepped off the plane in China." They went on to thank the relocation counselor for sending them to the training session where they played *BaFa BaFa*. They felt that the game had helped them recognize their reactions to change and to learn that they had control over themselves, but not over every situation. As they concluded in their letter, "The Chinese will be Chinese and have been for centuries—but we are finding that we can manage our reactions to the cultural differences."

Cultural adjustment issues can be dealt with in other ways. Families need to deal with each aspect of transition: saying good-bye; identifying persons, places, and things they will miss; being in limbo; settling into the new culture; establishing new support networks; and connecting to their new community. Families can be helped to prepare for culture shock with reading materials and discussion based on their specific needs, concerns, and interests. Intercultural exercises can also help families prepare for the ways that overseas life can cause discomfort.

Cultural adjustment sessions also provide opportunities for discussing a frequent response under stress—that is, "they" (in this case, the foreign culture) are to blame for everything. This scapegoating is found within families too. But Beavers observed that in healthy families, the members do not scapegoat each other. When scapegoating occurs, the counselor needs to intervene. For example, when Susie (in the Smith family mentioned previously) complained that all their problems began when her father was assigned overseas, the counselor legitimized Susie's feeling that life had been disrupted for this family, encouraged her to talk about the losses she was facing, and helped the family support her. She also referred the family to a workshop where they played *BaFa BaFa* with other families, and the peer support (so important to a teenager) that Susie received brought about an improvement in her attitude.

Transcendent values of the family are another variable from the Beavers model that relate to successful cultural adjustment. In talking about change, families often become aware in new ways of the values in which they believe. The therapist or trainer can be a catalyst for this awareness by highlighting the values statements and beliefs that are apt to sustain the family in time of change.

Communication

Trainers and therapists can help family members develop skills they will need in order to communicate among themselves and with people of another culture. The internal communication links need to be strong because family members provide the primary support group for an uprooted family. Family members can help one another interpret events, interactions, and the like. Typically, each family member holds pieces of the cultural puzzle. By putting the pieces together, the family creates a much bigger and potentially more accurate picture of the culture. Exercises that can enhance families' internal communication skills include: critical incidents, role plays, listening skills practice, and problem-solving scenarios. Each exercise affords opportunities to reinforce functioning of healthy boundaries, contextual clarity, power issues, autonomy, and affective issues.

For example, the Foreign Service Institute (FSI) uses a role play in their Going Overseas Workshop that is based on Virginia Satir's work (1972). Trainers at FSI have found that many families experience a communication breakdown during stress, particularly when adjusting to a new culture. Rehearsal can help family members resist the strong tendency to attack one another and create distance between themselves just when they most need one another. The role play scenario has a husband coming home from a good day of work at the embassy and his wife greeting him with anger because she was verbally assaulted when she bumped a foreign national's car while parking. Various responses by the husband are tried out corresponding to Satir's maladaptive ways of responding. For example, the "distractor" says everything will be all right, the "computer" tries to analyze the situation, and the "blamer" tells his wife to be more careful. Couples are then encouraged to try alternatives that really help the situation, such as responding empathetically to how the wife is feeling about the incident. Finally, couples are encouraged to generalize beyond the role play to practice empathetic responses to real-life situations. Trainers who are familiar with the Beavers model could also point out links between this exercise and the parental coalition, and power and structure issues in the family. They would also want to be sure that couples are aware of the special importance of warm communication and the negative effect of distancing during the distress of culture shock.

The ability to communicate in a foreign language is a key to living in and learning about a new culture. Families can be encouraged to acquire new language skills and can be taught how to gather data in a foreign culture by using an exercise that asks participants to evaluate the various sources of information available in their target culture. A language-learning game that works well with individual families, but even better with groups of families, is *Piglish* (Youth for Understanding, 1985). It was developed by Youth for Understanding to help exchange students learn about learning language. Families can have a lot of fun with the game which involves learning a new language and working out how to tell the story of the three little pigs in *Piglish*. Since language is often learned more quickly by the young, this exercise can create a situation in which the children develop more power than the parents. By mirroring this real-world experience, the game offers an excellent opportunity for families to work with power shifts under pressure.

Culture-Specific Information

People going into another culture often want a list of "do's and don'ts." Whether or not such a list would actually prove useful, providing culture-specific information is important and satisfies a strong need. There are some interesting ways to get the information across. One of the best is to find an appropriate family from the host culture and create a comfortable opportunity for the two families to meet. Other ways include films, ethnic meals, and field trips. During these sessions there should also be some discussion of family-specific topics such as the hypothetical or real illness of an elderly grandparent, adolescent needs, or the family pet. Asking the family to write an essay on the host culture by using resources at hand gets everyone involved because even the youngest ones can draw pictures to illustrate the essay. It also gets each family member accustomed to looking up needed information.

Culture-specific work often affords unexpected opportunities. During one family's preparation for India, the family was working with a relocation counselor who chose a book of colorful pictures for them to look at together. The counselor asked five-year-old Lisa about a picture of an old woman dressed in traditional Indian garb. Lisa identified the old woman as a very scary old witch and then announced she wasn't going to go any place where there were witches! The counselor encouraged Lisa to talk about witches and through a long discussion and a series of questions helped the child distinguish between her idea of witches and the different ways people look in other parts of the world. The counselor not only helped work through a potential problem, but modeled for the parents an effective way of addressing their daughter's fears. This counselor also worked on the concept of conceptual clarity. Beavers noted that optimal families do not stereotype each other, and in this extension of that concept, Lisa and her parents were shown some of the limitations of stereotyping outside the family as well.

The process by which a family learns about a new culture should ideally tap into all eight variables in the Beavers model and provide many intervention points to reinforce and encourage healthy family functioning. Using this training framework in concert with the Beavers model to prepare families for intercultural adjustment and the challenge of culture shock can make a notable difference in the ability of families to successfully manage the experience of living overseas.

Conclusion

A family's adjustment to a new country is clearly affected by many factors such as the country of placement and that culture's ideas about the family, gender roles, and children. These factors must be addressed in any comprehensive relocation training or counseling program. However, the goal of this chapter has been to introduce one particular theory of healthy family dynamics to see how it can assist counselors or trainers working with intact families to prepare and support them in their adjustment to living in another culture.

As those whose professional focus is cultural transitions discover, one of the greatest challenges in working with families who are adjusting to living and working in another culture is to go beyond simply providing the support required to meet their pragmatic needs and immediate concerns. The model presented here can help clinicians and trainers who wish to have both a theoretical base and a model for day-to-day decisions in counseling and training. Many kinds of models can be used to integrate theory and practice. Whether or not one agrees with Beavers' definition of a healthy family, the Beavers model emphasizes the family as a system which can attain optimal functioning. This is a goal we want the families we work with to achieve.

Much can be learned from focusing on this particular model for family functioning as a means of understanding the dynamics of any given family in depth. Other models might be more successful with certain types of family pathology, with families from non-American cultures, or with families facing stressors other than cultural adjustment. Although the authors believe that the Beavers model works well for helping families manage the complexities of intercultural relocation, counselors and trainers must find a model that fits their personal style and conviction.

At this time there are no empirical studies favoring one model over another. Such studies need to be undertaken so that relocation counselors and trainers can be more sure of the outcome of their work and more precise in their reinforcement strategies. Until family systems theory and intercultural practice are more empirically linked, we must continue to critically evaluate our results. Perhaps more importantly, we need to lay the groundwork for the future by linking theory and practice in the work we do.

Note: The material presented in this chapter derives from the authors' experience in developing a workshop for trainers and mental health professionals who are involved in helping families cope with the stresses of culture shock. The workshop was conducted most recently at the International Counseling Center's Second Annual Conference on Cross-Cultural Transitions. Robbins Hopkins, ProSources, was a major contributor to the design and delivery of the initial workshops.

References

Adler, N. J. (1986). *International dimensions of organizational behavior.* Boston: Kent Publishing Company.

Barna, L. M. (1983). The stress factor in intercultural relations. In D. Landis & R. W. Brislin (Eds.), *Handbook of intercultural training: Vol. II, Issues in training methodology* (pp. 19-49). New York: Pergamon Press.

Beavers, W. R. (1977). *Psychotherapy and growth: A family systems perspective.* New York: Brunner/Mazel.

Bower, E. M. (1967). American children and families in overseas communities. *American Journal of Orthopsychiatry, 37,* 787-796.

Cleveland, H., & Mangone, G. J. (1957). *The art of overseasmanship.* Syracuse, NY: Syracuse University Press.

Copeland, L., & Griggs, L. (1985). *Going international.* New York: Random House.

David, H. P., & Elkind, D. (1966). Family adaptation overseas. *Mental hygiene, 50*(1).

Fowler, S. M. (1985, October). *Prevention and assistance: Mobilizing the family for overseas assignment.* Paper presented at the meeting of the Guy's/Charter Third Annual Symposium on Expatriate Stress, London.

Golin, A. E. (1963). *Evaluating programs and personnel overseas: A review of methods and practices.* New York: Columbia University Bureau of Applied Research.

Grove, C. L., & Torbiorn, I. (1985) A new conceptualization of intercultural adjustment and the goals of training. *International Journal of Intercultural Relations, 9*(2), 205-235.

Gurin, J. (1985, October). The us generation. *American Health,* pp. 39-41.
Guthrie, G. M., & McKendry, M. (1964, August). *Predicting performance in a new culture.* Paper presented at the meeting of the American Psychological Association, Los Angeles, CA.
Kaslow, F. W. (1981). Profile of the healthy family. *Fokus pa Familian [Norwegian Journal of Family Therapy],* 1980, *Interaction* (Spring-Summer), 1981, 4(1&2), 1-15.
McCubbin, H. I., Joy, C. B., Cauble, A. E., Comeau, J. K., Patterson, J. M., & Needle, R. H. (1980). *Family stress and coping decade review.* Project funded by the Agriculture Experiment Station, University of Minnesota, St. Paul.
Meichenbaum, D. (1985). *Stress inoculation training.* New York: Pergamon Press.
Paige, R. M. (Ed.). (1986). *Cross-cultural orientation: New conceptualizations and applications.* Lanham, MD: University Press of America.
Piet-Pelon, N. J., & Hornby, B. (1985). *In another dimension: A guide for women who live overseas.* Yarmouth, ME: Intercultural Press.
Reiss, D., & Oliveri, M. E. (1982). Family paradigm and family coping: A proposal for linking the family's intrinsic adaptive capacities to its responses to stress. In F. W. Kaslow (Ed.), *The international book of family therapy* (pp. 95-119). New York: Brunner/Mazel.
Rigamer, E. F. (1985). Stresses of families abroad. *Travel Medicine International, 3*(3), 137-140.
Satir, V. (1972). *Peoplemaking.* Palo Alto, CA: Science and Behavior Books.
Shirts, R. G. (1973). *BaFa BaFa: A Cross-Culture Simulation.* Del Mar, CA: Simile II.
Torbiorn, I. (1982). *Living abroad: Personal adjustment and personnel policy in the overseas setting.* Chichester, England: John Wiley and Sons.
Torre, M. (Ed.). (1963). *The selection of personnel for international service.* New York: World Federation for Mental Health.
Wallach, J., & Metcalf, G. (1981, Summer). Raising children overseas. *The Bridge,* pp. 13-14.
Weaver, G. R. (1986). Understanding and coping with cross-cultural adjustment stress. In R. M. Paige (Ed.), *Cross-cultural orientation: New conceptualizations and applications* (pp. 111-147). Lanham, MD: University Press of America.
Werkman, S. (1977). *Bringing up children overseas: A guide for families.* New York: Basic Books.
Youth for Understanding and Training Resources Group. (1985). *Piglish: Intercultural Communication Skills.* Washington, DC: Youth for Understanding.

Chapter 9

Organizational Factors in Cross-Cultural Counseling
David J. Bachner and Sharon K. Rudy

This chapter proposes a framework for understanding the forces and dynamics which affect cross-cultural counseling processes in organizational settings. The need for such a framework rests on the premise that a counselor's ability to manage the counselor-organization interface will have a direct and important bearing on that counselor's effectiveness in providing services to cross-cultural clients. The framework itself is applicable to a range of organizational settings in which cross-cultural counselors are likely to work, including exchange programs, universities, volunteer agencies, and government bureaus. While the focus of this chapter is on the professional counselor's role in helping across cultures, other roles in a helping system, including those of paraprofessionals and management, are also addressed.

In developing this framework, we have drawn heavily from organizational theory and systems perspectives in the belief that:

1. a substantial number of clients are subject to assistance by cross-cultural counselors who work for organizations and institutions;
2. cross-cultural counseling as a field has attended in both theory and practice to more dyadic (i.e., counselor-client) issues than organizational and systemic issues;
3. the cross-cultural counseling relationship is often subject to complex realities and influences beyond the scope of the counseling relationship itself;
4. these realities are inherent to the broader organizational and institutional contexts within which counseling occurs; and
5. a knowledge of contextual factors can do much to enhance the effectiveness of cross-cultural counseling by generating comprehensive definitions of the counseling problem, realistic expectations of what institutionally based counseling can achieve, and multidimensional counseling strategies.

These assumptions are elaborated upon in three sections. The chapter begins by discussing the need for more systemic approaches to cross-cultural counseling and notes the relevance of general systems theory in addressing this need. The second section posits five groups of factors which the authors believe can help cross-cultural counselors understand and work with organizational forces. These factors are then used to examine the organizational dynamics which come into play during an actual cross-cultural counseling situation involving a foreign exchange student. The final section looks at implications that the framework may offer for further application in the cross-cultural counseling field.

Institutional Settings and the Systems Perspective

Approximately 350,000 foreign students and scholars are currently studying at universities in the United States. Tens of thousands of secondary school students from abroad also visit this country each year as participants in private exchange programs which include study and/or homestay components. Many recent immigrants are being helped to adjust to life in this country through "mainstreaming" programs conducted by community institutions. At the same time, thousands of American students and scholars at any given time are living abroad, as are large numbers of diplomats, business people, military personnel, technical advisors, and their dependents.

Because of the difficulties inherent in cross-cultural adjustment, a substantial proportion of these sojourners (both here and abroad) benefit from special assistance. Both exchange students and others who are abroad under the auspices of an organization typically receive such assistance in institutional settings. This implies that help is available to them in the context of an organizational counseling system where expectations, rules, and procedures of the institution lie outside the control of the immediate counselor-client relationship. In many instances, the organizational setting is cross-cultural, as in the case of international exchange programs or business organizations with multinational operations that have internationally coordinated support systems. In many other instances, as in the case of help available to foreign students at an American university through a foreign-student advisory office, the counselor-client relationship itself will entail interaction between people of different cultural backgrounds. Moreover, this relationship exists within the cross-cultural context of the university at large as represented in differing perspectives among departments and disciplines.

Cross-cultural counseling in an organizational setting, then, represents an undertaking of considerable and often unrecognized complexity. For the most part, research and theory have focused more on dyadic (i.e., counselor-client) complexity than on systemic (i.e., organizational and institutional) complexity. This is ironic since the field of cross-cultural counseling is fundamentally contextual and systemic in its emphasis on the conditioning influence of roles, values, communication patterns, behaviors, rituals, and the like. Counseling, which has aptly been characterized as "a counselor-client coalition against the problem. . ." (Pedersen, 1976), needs as a field to put more stress on what constitutes the limits, or salient dimensions, of "the problem" and to consider the power of context in defining the problem and its effect on possible solutions.

Within the cross-cultural counseling literature, however, there are exceptions to the general trend to isolate individuals and dyads from the systems in which they operate. These exceptions can be found under various rubrics, including "person-environment transaction" (see, for example, Ivey, 1981), "community psychology" (Rappaport, 1977), and "ecological psychology" (Moos & Insell, 1974). Moos and Insell, as well as Sundberg (1977), are especially notable in their emphasis on the need to consider a range of systemic variables in cross-cultural counseling assessment and intervention.

Conceptually, these works are the descendants of open-systems models (e.g., Bertalanffy, 1950; Hawley, 1950; Homans, 1950; and more recently, Pasmore & Sherwood, 1978; and Ackoff, 1981) which emphasize the constant interaction and functional interdependence between organisms (individual and aggregate) and their environments. The value of the systems perspective for cross-cultural counseling is its explicit recognition that the counseling dyad and the counseling process are not fully autonomous units: that is, the main actors cannot completely control which outside forces will impinge upon them or how those forces may influence the counselor-client relationship. There is, in other words, an interaction between the counseling relationship and its environment which should not be ignored; moreover, the source of many problems or issues encountered in the relationship may be seen to lie outside the formal parameters of the counselor-client relationship itself.

This recognition is particularly important because so many cross-cultural counseling relationships exist within institutional settings. These settings add a complexity and dynamism that go well beyond those which are at play in a strictly defined dyadic relationship. The complexity arises from the seemingly infinite number of variables affecting an organizational sphere of action; the dynamism arises from the constant interaction of these variables. If an institutionally based counseling process is to be consistently effective, the organizational variables most likely to affect it must be adequately considered. In many cases, it is only when these organizational factors have been accounted for that meaningful intervention and helping strategies can be put in motion.

Framework and Application

In this section, the situation of Keiko, an 18-year-old Japanese exchange student to the United States, provides an opportunity to build upon the systems perspective in examining how an actual cross-cultural counseling situation may be influenced by organizational forces.

In describing Keiko's situation, five sets of factors are analyzed: (1) forces within individuals, (2) forces within the task, (3) forces within management, (4) forces within history, and (5) forces within the environment. These five factors reflect not only the analysis of Keiko's situation but various categorization schemes suggested in the literature of organizational theory (see especially Shetty & Carlisle, 1972). Taken together, they offer a simple yet comprehensive framework for identifying relevant phenomena and understanding the interplay of those phenomena.

Forces Within Individuals

The situation. Keiko came to the United States on full scholarship in an academic-year exchange program administered by one of the long-established high school exchange organizations. A major feature of this organization is its reliance on volunteers, both as host families and as area representatives supporting program participants. A sizable staff guides and provides resources to these volunteers in their work with students and families.

Keiko had been transferred out of her first host family after extensive consultation with the area representative (AR). Everyone had been optimistic that the second family would work out well until the family phoned the AR to request the girl's removal. Despite the family's efforts to help the student adjust, Keiko seemed depressed, withdrawn, and unusually morbid. According to the host mother, Keiko spent all of her time in her room either studying her American high school lessons or Japanese books and participated little with the family. The family had discovered several poems that the girl had written which seemed to glorify suicide. The school counselor reported that Keiko was doing well academically, but was usually seen alone between class periods and apparently had no friends. Her English teacher had expressed concern because the theme of death and dying kept appearing in Keiko's written work.

The concerns which this family expressed echoed those of Keiko's first host family. The AR, who was trained in helping with cross-cultural transitions, had initially thought that Keiko was suffering from culture shock and simply needed a more suitable family match. The AR described Keiko as respectful, cooperative, shy, and very creative. However, with the apparent failure of the second placement, the AR felt not only concern for the student but also embarrassment over the situation. He had located both families from among his own circle of acquaintances and felt guilty that he had let the families down. He was irritated that Keiko could not seem to adjust to the reasonable demands and expectations of the American families and the exchange program.

Keiko, in the meantime, was having a very difficult experience in the United States, particularly in coping with her terrible loneliness. She was a sensitive person from an artistic family whose thinking reflected the value placed by the Japanese on endurance as a means of strengthening the spirit; she was actually proud of how well she had been surviving the rigors of living with an American family. Keiko believed she had been kind and respectful to her host families, particularly when she refused to criticize what she considered their rude behavior to the AR. Keiko was only as interested in death as she was in the meaning of life, and saw the act of suicide from her family's traditional point of view—as an honorable option which enhances the family's reputation, particularly in a situation where there is potential for loss of face.

Feeling pressure to resolve the situation, the AR approached Keiko with some anxiety and irritation. He described the behaviors which were unacceptable to the families; he pointed out repeated complaints and attempted to reason with the student, moving quickly to encourage the student to verbalize her remorse and willingness to adjust. He was disappointed with Keiko's failure to see how she was being perceived by others.

Finally, frustrated by his inability to resolve the situation, the AR referred the entire matter to the staff of the exchange student organization who were, after all, paid to handle this kind of thing. The AR told the organization's regional support coordinator that he was not willing or able to place the student in a third home. Keiko was referred to the regional counseling professional who lived in the vicinity.

Observations on individual factors. At this point, it is worth noting the various individuals' needs at work in the situation as described thus far. Then the power of those needs in influencing events can be recognized whether they result in reinforcement of or opposition to organizational policies and ends.

The AR had become involved in the student exchange organization after a successful and happy year of hosting another exchange student. Although the AR was sincerely committed to the friendship-through-exchange mission of the organization and its official philosophy of helping students adjust, several circumstances influenced his decision not to continue supporting Keiko. First, it was easier for the AR to identify with the host parents than with Keiko because he had more in common with the host families. They were members of the same community, of the same generation, and shared the same culture and language. Both host families were recruited from the AR's own circle of acquaintances, and they also had similar socioeconomic status and religious affiliations. Thus while the AR certainly wanted to help Keiko, he was constrained by his more natural empathy with the host families.

The AR's subjective reactions—that of embarrassment with his own loss of face among the families and others who knew of the problems, along with his irritation with Keiko for not adjusting well—had an impact on his patience, his efforts to appreciate Keiko's perceptions of events, and his ability to understand the internal forces which were causing Keiko to behave as she was. These reactions affected the decision-making process in this situation. The AR was supposed to make placement decisions in consultation with the regional support coordinator, who in turn could make a referral to the counselor. In this case, however, the AR essentially made the decision to refer the student for counseling by virtue of his refusal to consider a third placement. Whether or not assessment by a counselor was appropriate, the regional office had no alternative but to accept the case because of the AR's unilateral stance.

Another individual force influencing this situation was Keiko's cultural background and its impact on her behavior in the United States. Although her behavior caused concern among the American host families, she was content in the knowledge that her real parents perceived her to be a normal Japanese daughter who, by studying hard, was fulfilling her primary obligation to them. As an exchange student on a specially awarded competitive scholarship, Keiko was more concerned with her academic performance and her family's reputation in their community in Japan than she was with the more abstract goals and policies of the exchange program.

Behavioral models of organization make frequent reference to the importance of individual needs and motivations (e.g., Argyris, 1964; Herzberg, 1966). Such forces take on increased complexity as the number of parties involved grows and as the needs among these parties conflict. Keiko's situation was certainly subject to the difficulties posed by the conflicting needs of the parties involved.

Forces Within the Task

The situation (continued). Keiko was referred to a mental health professional retained by the exchange organization for referral as needed. The counselor met several times with Keiko and expressed some concern regarding the student's denial that there were problems with her adjustment, although the student did recognize that her host families had been disappointed in her. The counselor also reported that although the student was not suicidal, she did seem unusually preoccupied with death. However, the counselor felt that, given the student's traditional Japanese background, she had made significant efforts to adjust and, at least from the student's perspective, had made a number of difficult compromises. In light of the possibility that the loss of face from an early return might be devastating to Keiko's Japanese family and would be more likely to precipitate a suicidal crisis than if she stayed in the United States, however difficult that might be, the counselor recommended that the student be allowed to remain in the program. The counselor further recommended that Keiko be placed with a family who would understand and accept her priorities, her lack of interaction with others, and her tendency toward morbidity. The counselor also thought that Keiko would benefit from continued counseling support.

The counselor's recommendations notwithstanding, the manager of the exchange organization's regional office recommended to the headquarters review committee that Keiko return early to Japan. She felt that the full scope of the organization's support services had been utilized and there was no reasonable expectation that Keiko would do any better if placed with yet another family. She also wanted to support the AR, who had an excellent reputation, was a valued recruiter of families, and had made clear he didn't want to place Keiko with a third family in his area. Additionally, the regional manager thought the counselor, who had seen Keiko for only two sessions, may have been underestimating the seriousness of Keiko's fascination with death and dying.

On the other hand, the exchange organization's Japanese office presented a view of the student's behavior as culturally appropriate and normal in light of her traditional family environment in Japan.

Observations on task factors. Task, or the technologies and approaches by which an organization goes about its work, has been a common focus of concern and study around which a significant empirical literature has developed (see Woodward, 1965; Perrow, 1967; Thompson, 1967). Tensions inevitably exist in organizations as to the most effective and appropriate ways of pursuing organizational ends. Perceptions of what constitutes an organization's "real" and most important tasks are rarely uniform, and this lack of uniformity was certainly at play in Keiko's case.

The AR and the regional manager saw Keiko's continuation with the program in ways which were influenced by pressures contained in their respective organizational tasks—for the AR, keeping families happy and willing to cooperate in the future; for the manager, making sure that the organization's resources were not overextended in a questionable effort for one student. For the counselor, the professional task exerted an entirely different set of pressures which were at odds with certain other task-related perspectives, but which somehow had to come to terms with those perspectives. The counselor in this case was an experienced mental health professional who brought to the job not only her clinical skills but a code of professional ethics and a set of work habits. For the counselor to be perceived as competent, however, these skills, code, and style were necessarily subject to compromise or accommodation to institutional realities of working. In Keiko's case, the pacing of the assessment, counselor-client confidentiality, client advocacy, and the number of options available to the counselor when making recommendations were all affected by the counselor's role in the organization.

The counselor technically worked for the organization, not for the counselees. She therefore was in the position of having to work within a framework of existing policies and procedures which were designed to meet the needs of a large number of students, not just Keiko's. Moreover, confidentiality was defined on a need-to-know basis and, as a representative of the organization, the counselor had to define the relationship with the student from the beginning to prevent conflicts regarding information given by the student which should not be withheld from the organization.

The counselors in this organization were also seen as consultants who stood apart from the pressures of recruitment and public relations. Insofar as they had no placement responsibilities and only made recommendations, it was felt they were more likely to make recommendations that were in a student's best interest. Thus, although they were representatives of the organization when working with the student, they were also able to represent the student to the organization.

As a counselor becomes socialized into any organization, he or she comes to terms with the realities of organizational life, including the tension which exists for such internal consultants. In this specific support system, although the counselors remained officially separate from recruitment and public relations functions, they were not in fact immune to such realities, especially as they developed relationships with their colleagues at the regional office. Counselors were often acutely aware of those instances when their recommendations put pressure on staff concerning use of placement resources. In the case of Keiko, the counselor recommended that Keiko remain in the program because she felt it would be in the student's best interest and judged that the student's inner resources would help her bear up until she could return to Japan honorably. There may have been some subtle pressure on the counselor to make a different recommendation since she undoubtedly knew the wishes of the regional manager, who after all was her supervisor.

The regional manager, however, faced with such realities as the need for volunteer retention and the organization's local reputation, recommended Keiko's early return. From her vantage point, other considerations took precedence over the individual student's needs as defined by the counselor. The regional manager was more likely to be judged successful if she recruited adequate numbers of volunteers, host families, and students to go overseas. She cared about Keiko's experience, but, forced to prioritize, other tasks were simply more important.

Forces Within Management

The situation (continued). It was up to the headquarters review committee to make a final decision regarding Keiko based on the reports from the regional office, the counselor, and the Japanese national office. Three considerations were pivotal in their deliberations: the various assessments of Keiko's behavior, the amount of resources that would have to be expended, and the potential reactions of Keiko's scholarship sponsors.

Everyone agreed that Keiko's behavior would be difficult for an average American host family to accommodate, but there were different interpretations with respect to the meaning and significance of the behavior. The host families, the AR, and the regional manager believed that the behavior was intolerable in an exchange situation. The Japanese office, Keiko's natural parents, and the student herself defined the behavior as culturally normal, particularly given the stressful circumstances of overseas living.

There was also a difference of opinion regarding the reasonable limits of the organization's resources to be expended upon one student. On the one hand, the regional manager and AR felt that "using up" two host families plus plenty of volunteer support and professional counseling was enough. If no change could be promised, the student should return home early. On the other hand, the student was highly motivated to stay and would probably continue to make small changes; also, the counselor reported that the student was not a current suicide threat but might become suicidal in the event of an early return. Surely, the committee reasoned, there must be a family somewhere in the United States who could accept Keiko.

Finally, the review committee was concerned about the impact an early return might have on the important scholarship program funded by the U.S. government in which Keiko was participating. The concern was heightened by the prospect that the Japanese office, which had already expressed their view of Keiko's normality, would have difficulty articulating the reasons for her early return to the Japanese government, which was of course concerned that students in the United States under official auspices do well.

In the end, the committee unanimously agreed to place the student in yet a third family and to ensure her close access to a counselor.

Observations on management factors. The combination of individual and task factors involved in Keiko's case posed a fairly representative set of circumstances for the headquarters review committee. This committee was composed of the regional manager's supervisor, the program officer responsible for representing Japan, and the organization's director of counseling, who had professional (versus line) supervisory responsibility for the referral counselor who had worked with Keiko.

As a group, the committee, was responsible—and perceived itself as empowered—to resolve the conflicting individual needs and task perspectives and decide on a course of action that would be in the best interests of the organization and Keiko herself. As individuals, however, the committee members were understandably concerned with—and probably most sympathetic to—the points of view of the individuals under their respective spheres of supervision.

In a dyadic counseling relationship, decisions hinge largely on professional judgment. In Keiko's situation, the counselor's professional judgment was only one data element in a complex set of organizational considerations. As it turned out, the counselor's recommendations were followed in this case. Nevertheless, the committee's rationale for adopting that course of action was based as much on logistical, cost, and political considerations as it was on the counselor's psychological assessments.

In effect, as a member of the review committee, the director of counseling had to give equal attention to the counseling and noncounseling dimensions of the situation in order to sustain long-term credibility and effectiveness as a decision maker. Thus to *manage* the counseling process, as opposed to serving as a counselor, the director had to attend to varied organizational interests. Although occasionally at odds with the counseling director's individual needs and the strictest standards of conduct in the counseling profession, the requirements of the larger organization—including the requirement that decision makers render "right" and balanced judgments—dictated a *quid pro quo* approach to management. Practical success in the institutional setting frequently seems to require such trade-offs and return of favors.

Forces Within the Organization's History

The situation (continued). Organizations are formed by individuals, groups, or edicts to pursue certain purposes. A particular way of going about business develops, which in effect becomes the organization's personality. This personality can go through permutations, but there is a definite legacy which is likely to remain influential throughout the organization's existence. To a very large and frequently unrecognized extent, individual needs, task requirements, and managerial approaches are affected, if not actually caused, by an organization's historical legacy. Without understanding these forces, the counselor who works in an organizational setting is at a distinct disadvantage.

The counseling structure of the exchange program in which Keiko was a participant evolved from a very centralized system of support. The founder and first president of the organization counseled students informally in her office. It was considered normal for a student to need some help in adjusting, and it was seen as the responsibility of the sponsoring organization to ensure that assistance was provided. Organizational policies and procedures were developed as a framework to provide the greatest support to the greatest number of students and yet allow for flexibility in recognition of the intercultural nature of the organization and its multinational participant base.

For the first 20 years of the exchange program, the student participants were supported by a growing network of volunteer area representatives and then, if necessary, were referred to the headquarters office for a talk with the president. During the organization's third decade, a new president introduced an additional layer to the support system by hiring professional counselors to see students before a referral was made to the headquarters office. With the counselors came the concept of specialization and the beginning of the decentralization of counseling services in the organization.

In the early 1980s, under the organization's third president, further decentralization of the counseling role occurred as students no longer were referred to the central office at all for counseling. Instead, all counseling was done regionally. At this point, the focus of the headquarters counseling department changed. It now attempted to ensure that the decentralized components of the support system maintained a given quality of service to program participants, while at the same time increasing the caliber of documentation of cases and standardizing policies and procedures to increase consistency throughout the system.

The support system at work in Keiko's situation was a product of a 35-year evolution from a centralized, nonspecialized, and informal structure to a structure which featured considerable decentralization, specialization, and formal parameters for the provision of counseling services. The resulting system, composed as it was of volunteers, professional counselors, and paid staff with line responsibilities from a number of countries, required a high degree of coordination to manage the multiplicity of data sources, perspectives, and interests involved.

Observations on historical factors. The historical factor, or force, consists of four central elements, namely: an organization's mission, leadership, memory, and culture. Each of these elements had a distinct impact on the way in which the exchange program participants, including Keiko, were supported.

Different leaders convey and oversee direction with different styles. A leader who delegates will set up a different kind of expectation than a leader who retains full authority. Rarely will leadership be consistent across generations: approaches differ, and so do degrees of influence. However, one generation's leadership will influence the next, and the totality of leaders will leave an aggregate mark on the organization. In Keiko's case, the background, knowledge, experience, values, and style of each president, past and present, influenced the manner in which she was supported. The first president chose a very personal approach, which continued despite its inefficiency once the organization outgrew its infancy. However, the president's personal interest in counseling students set limits on the structure of support. The second president encouraged a more independent counseling staff. The decision-making authority became less centralized during this period and the headquarters counselor (rather than the president) made the final decision regarding any student's dismissal from the program. Moreover, this president's emphasis on growth and professionalism within the organization led to an expanded, credentialed staff as more students were recruited for the program.

A second historical element which was influential in Keiko's situation was the actual mission of the organization (i.e., to promote world peace and understanding by providing host family experiences for teenagers in other cultures and nations). Missions are frequently subject to interpretation, depending on circumstances and leadership at any given time. However, there is generally an essential premise, stated or implied, that is an immutable part of any organization's mission. The core premise influencing Keiko's case was that it would be in everyone's best interest if as many students as possible were helped to stay for the full term of their program.

The third element of an organization's history is the recollection or memory of that history. An organization's collective memory—be it accurate or inaccurate—has the power of myth and influences greatly the way things operate and the way events are perceived. In Keiko's case, none of the review committee members had even been with the organization when the premise took root. Yet they were all subject to its influence in a kind of moral imperative which directly, if subtly, affected their decision. Had Keiko been sent home early, the committee members undoubtedly would have felt that they had failed to measure up to the organization's mandate as it existed, unstated but nevertheless real, in everyone's memory.

Finally, the culture within the organization also affected the support system and the manner in which students, including Keiko, were counseled. Certain norms and behaviors involving participation, delegation, consultation, and compromise had been crystallized into a characteristic way of working over time. As the organization evolved, for example, the headquarters office had become increasingly professionalized. The credentialed counseling staff tended to identify more closely with their professional associates in other settings than they did with the volunteer area representatives in the field. This dichotomy between the volunteers and the professional counselors was heightened by the decentralization of direct service counseling into the field. The role of the clinical staff at the headquarters was no longer face-to-face counseling but rather training, consultation, and coordination of counseling services. Although decision making had become more decentralized, a student's dismissal from the program continued to rest with a review committee in the headquarters office.

Forces Within the Environment

The situation (concluded). It has already been noted that Keiko was a scholarship student and that her sponsor was the U.S. government. Not surprisingly, this special status was taken into consideration by the review committee in deciding whether Keiko would continue in the program. In fact, this consideration was a powerful one for several related reasons.

First, there was the practical issue of support, both monetary and official. In a world of limited resources, particularly for such "nonessential" activities as student exchange, attracting and then sustaining funding are essential to an organization's survival. Also, the *de facto* endorsement that the exchange organization had acquired by being chosen to administer this government-sponsored program increased its prospects not only for continued funding of that particular program, but for similar funding and similar recognition by other sponsors, governmental and otherwise. Conversely, losing such a program might have been seen, in Japan and elsewhere, as an expression of lost confidence in the organization's ability to administer that and perhaps other programs. It is unlikely that Keiko's case alone would have resulted in such losses, but this possibility was surely on the minds of the review committee, and, in particular, the program officer representing Japan.

The second reason for concern was competition within the exchange field. A number of organizations were and are active in the field. Each seeks competitive advantage over the others in attracting participants, support, and recognition. Thus the fear of losing a program was not limited to direct funding and endorsement issues, but reflected the need to maintain the organization's place within the exchange field generally. On the other hand, the regional manager had made a case for the potential loss of reputation in the school, community, and among volunteers if a "problem student" was allowed to remain in the program.

Finally, there was the influence of regulatory exposure. While this was not a pivotal factor in the decision, it was nonetheless a consideration in the minds of the committee members. The causal chain of that thinking is instructive in understanding the forces that often affect institutionally based counseling processes: (1) Keiko is a foreign student who (2) represents the government of Japan through (3) U.S. government funding. Therefore, (4) she will be more visible than most students and (5) we do not want any aspect of her support—placement, replacement, volunteer assistance, or counseling assistance—to be seen as inadequate in any way. So, (6) since the grounds for early return contain a certain margin of doubt, (7) we'll keep her in the program.

Observations on environmental factors. In systems terms, an organization's effectiveness depends on its ability to adjust to the requirements of both its internal components and its relevant external surroundings—that is, the environmental aspects which most affect it (see Beer, 1980; Burns & Stalker, 1961; Emery & Trist, 1965; and Galbraith, 1970). The high degree of uncertainty and instability in most organizational environments today makes such adjustments difficult and multidimensional.

As Keiko's situation helps demonstrate, the exchange organization had to cope with such market variables as resource availability and competition for existing resources. It had to adjust to political realities as well, both internationally (Japanese-U.S. relations) and operationally as reflected in the current regulatory mood of the U.S. government with respect to student exchange (which in turn may have been precipitated by such larger environmental issues as the general public's adverse reaction to increased immigration).

In any event, the conduct of the counseling process was to some extent a function of forces beyond the more obvious confines of the specific counselor-client situation.

The Counselor as Tactician

The counselor who works in an institutional setting has a duty to three different entities: the person with whom he or she is in a counseling relationship, the counseling profession itself, and the organization. The weight, or significance, ascribed to each of the three relationships will vary from counselor to counselor, but it is likely that each will exert some measure of influence in most institutionally based counseling situations. To that extent, the counselor must be able to work with all three.

This article has proceeded from the assumption that much cross-cultural counseling is offered in an institutional setting and that the realities and needs of the organization in such situations are often not adequately recognized. By extension, a second assumption is that mental health practitioners often fail to function with optimum effectiveness in an institutional setting. A third assumption, to be addressed in this concluding section, is that practitioners can and should be prepared to work effectively in the context of an organizational setting.

We propose that this preparation incorporate three tracks, namely: developing a knowledge base about organizations generally, learning to apply this knowledge base to the understanding of particular organizations, and developing the ability to effectively manage the counseling process in an organizational setting.

Developing a Knowledge Base

Understanding organizational dynamics is a logical precursor to managing them. Keiko's case was discussed within a five-category scheme to demonstrate the ways in which individual, task, managerial, historical, and environmental factors affected a specific cross-cultural counseling process. The analysis of Keiko's situation was undertaken and the five factors applied from the authors' particular point of view about organizations, but the framework itself is sufficiently comprehensive to increase an observer's ability to understand what occurs in most organizations.

Diagnosing an Organization

Within the general categories cited, however, different organizations will manifest their dynamics in different ways. In Table 1, a diagnostic questionnaire presents these five factors in a format that should help practitioners apply this perspective to specific organizations.

The authors have several objectives in offering this series of questions. The first is to differentiate various dimensions within the five factors; depending on the organization and the individual examining the organization, certain dimensions will have more relevance than others. The second objective is to reinforce the idea that the five factors are complex and that, consequently, the pressures they exert on a counseling situation are also complex. The third objective is to represent the dimensions in practical, operational terms by expressing them as questions that can be considered in personal, nontechnical, and potentially implementable ways. Finally, it is assumed that effective action is preceded by understanding, which in turn depends on systematic reflection.

Table 1

Diagnostic Questionnaire for Counselors Working in Institutional Settings

1. Forces within the individual
   o What is important to you in your job?
   o What specific factors motivate you to do well?
   o What are the points of most common conflict as you do your job?
   o Who in your work setting has the most significant impact on your job?
   o How do you personally respond to these people and the pressure they represent?

2. Forces within the task
   o What precepts do you remember from your counseling training about what it means to be a counseling "professional"?
   o What professional standards do you consider to be currently compelling and relevant?
   o How would you define your professional identity?
   o What are the special qualities or unique aspects of your counseling setting?
   o How does your current setting affect your usual working style? In what ways have you needed to modify your typical working style, counseling

habits, or ethical code in order to work effectively in your current work
setting?

3. **Forces within management**
   o Which managers or administrators have the most impact on your work?
   o How would you describe each manager's basic philosophical perspective
     about organizational needs and assumptions about supervision? About
     counseling?
   o What do you think is important for these individuals? How would they
     define success for themselves? How would they define success for others?
   o What conflicts do you think the administrators experience?
   o What forces do you think they are attempting to balance in their own
     jobs?

4. **Forces within the history**
   o Who has led the organization in the past?
   o For each leader, what was the predominant style of management?
   o How would you characterize the underlying philosophical approach and
     assumptions of each leader? Were there areas of commonality?
   o What major decisions did each leader make which continue to have an
     effect? List specific effects, especially on counseling.
   o What are the organization's milestones/important events/most often told
     stories about the past?
   o What would you list as the major rules (written and unwritten) of
     behavior in the organization?

5. **Forces within the environment**
   o What would you list as special aspects of the "world" in which your
     organization operates?
   o What are the underlying realities in the environment which are not
     changeable? What are the "givens"? What forces exert the greatest
     pressure?
   o What environmental demands are negotiable versus immutable?
   o How would you characterize or describe the market factors that determine
     organizational viability and, therefore, its essential tasks?
   o How would you describe your organization's resources and their
     availability? What does the organization have to do to maintain and
     protect those resources?
   o Are there outside forces involved in the regulation of your organization?
   o To whom is your organization accountable?
   o Whose interests does the organization have to respond to?
   o Which influences seem to affect counseling the most?

Conclusion

Increased understanding of organizations and the ability to specify relevant dynamics on the basis of that understanding are preconditions for the effective management of counseling processes within organizations. The actual act of management, however, requires additional skills in such areas as negotiation, conflict management, communication, group facilitation and decision making, consulting, and strategizing interventions.

In essence, counselors in an organizational setting need to function as involved, benevolent manipulators of organizational forces. The counselor role can be awkward, compromising, and subject to a variety of difficult, if not unresolvable, conflicts as the counselor attempts to balance the requirements of practicality and the standards of professional ethics.

It is, nonetheless, a role for which cross-cultural counselors who will work in institutional settings could and should be trained. At stake is their long-term individual effectiveness, as well as the ultimate effectiveness of cross-cultural counseling as a field centered increasingly within institutions.

References

Ackoff, R. L. (1981). *Creating the corporate future.* New York: John Wiley and Sons.

Argyris, C. (1964). *Integrating the individual and the organization.* New York: John Wiley and Sons.

Beer, M. (1980). *Organizational change and development: A systems view.* Pacific Palisades, CA: Goodyear.

Bertalanffy, L. von. (1950). The theory of open systems in physics and biology. *Science,* Vol. III, 23-29.

Burns, T., & Stalker, G. M. (1961). *The management of innovation.* London: Tavistock.

Emery, F. E., & Trist, E. L. (1965). The casual texture of organizational environments. *Human Relations, 18,* 21-23.

Galbraith, J. R. (1970). Environmental and technological determinants of organizational design. In J. W. Lorsch & P. R. Lawrence (Eds.), *Studies in organization design* (pp. 113-139). Homewood, IL: Richard D. Irwin.

Hawley, A. H. (1950). *Human ecology: A theory of community structure.* New York: Ronald Press.

Herzberg, F. (1966). *Work and the nature of man.* New York: World Publishing Co.

Homans, G. (1950). *The human group.* New York: Harcourt Brace.

Ivey, A. E. (1981). Counseling and psychotherapy: Toward a new perspective. In
A. J. Marsella & P. B. Pedersen (Eds.), *Cross-cultural counseling and
psychotherapy*. New York: Pergamon Press.

Moos, R., & Insell, P. (Eds.). (1974). *Issues in social ecology*. Palo Alto, CA:
Consulting Psychologists Press.

Pasmore, W. A., & Sherwood, J. J. (1978). *Sociotechnical systems: A source
book*. San Diego, CA: University Associates.

Pedersen, P., (1976). A cross-cultural triad training model for counselors.
Unpublished manuscript.

Perrow, C. (1967, April). A framework for the comparative analysis of
organizations. *American Sociology Review*, 194-208.

Rappaport, J. (1977). *Community psychology* New York: Holt, Rinehart and
Winston.

Shetty, Y. K., & Carlisle, H. M. (1972). A contingency model of organizational
design. *California Management Review, 15*(1), 38-45.

Sundberg, N. D. (1977). *Assessment of persons*. Englewood Cliffs, NJ:
Prentice-Hall.

Thompson, J. D. (1967). *Organizations in action*. New York: McGraw-Hill.

Woodward, J. (1965). *Industrial organization: Theory and practice*. Fairlawn, NJ:
Oxford University Press.